HINDU GODS AND GODDESSES

Swami Harshananda

SRI RAMAKRISHNA MATH
MYLAPORE, MADRAS 600 004

Published by
Adhyaksha
Sri Ramakrishna Math
Mylapore, Chennai-4

First Edition, October 1981
Second Edition, September 1982
Twenty-fourth Print, December 2014
2M3C

ISBN 81-7120-110-5

Total number of copies
printed till now: 90,500

Printed in India at
Sri Ramakrishna Math Printing Press
Mylapore, Chennai-4

sarvadevasvarūpasya
sarvadevīsvarūpiṇaḥ
arpitā rāmakṛṣṇasya
kṛtiḥ śrīcaraṇāmbuje

Dedicated at the holy lotus feet
of Bhagavān Śrī Rāmakṛṣṇa
who is the embodiment of all
gods and goddesses

Contents

LIST OF ILLUSTRATIONS

The illustrations are based on the images and sculptures obtaining in well-known temples and archaeological monuments. Wherever the description given in the text and the drawing do not match, it should be presumed that variations in form are allowed by the iconographical works.

KEY TO TRANSLITERATION

Roman	Devanāgarī	Roman	Devanāgarī
a	अ	ṭh	ठ
ā	आ	ḍ	ड
i	इ	ḍh	ढ
ī	ई	ṇ	ण
u	उ	t	त
ū	ऊ	th	थ
ṛ	ऋ	d	द
e	ए	dh	ध
ai	ऐ	n	न
o	ओ	p	प
au	औ	ph	फ
ṁ (anusvāra)	ं	b	ब
ḥ (visarga)	ः	bh	भ
k	क	m	म
kh	ख	y	य
g	ग	r	र
gh	घ	l	ल
ṅ	ङ	v	व
c	च	ś	श
ch	छ	ṣ	ष
j	ज	s	स
jh	झ	h	ह
ñ	ञ	jñ	ज्ञ
ṭ	ट		

BIBLIOGRAPHY

1. CHIDBHAVANANDA, Swami: Facets of Brahman or Hindu Gods (Tirupparaitturai, Sri Ramakrishna Tapovanam, 1974)
2. DANIELOU, Alain: Hindu Polytheism (New York, Bollingen Foundation, 1964)
3. GOPINATHA RAO, T.A.: Elements of Hindu Iconography, Vol. I-II Edn. 2 (Delhi, Motilal Banarsidass, 1968)
4. GUPTE, R.S.: Iconography of Hindus, Buddhists and Jains (Bombay, D.B. Taraporevala Sons & Co. 1972)
5. HARIDAS MITRA: Ganapati (Santiniketan, Calcutta, Visva-Bharati, (Reprint of Visva Bharati, Annals, Vol. VIII)
6. "INDU" INDERJIT: Science of Symbols: Deeper view of Indian Deities (New Delhi, Geetanjali Pulications, 1977)
7. KRISHNA SASTRI, H,: South Indian Images of Gods and Goddesses (Delhi, Bharatiya Publishing House, 1974)
8. RAMRAO, Benegal and SUNDARA SASTRY, Panyam: Purananama Chudamani (in Kannada) (Mysore, Prasaranga, Mysore University, 1977)
9. SRIDHARA MURTHY, M: Ganapati (in Kannada) (Bangalore, Rashtrotthana Sahitya, 1971.)
10. STUTLEY, Margaret and James: A Dictionary of Hinduism: Its Mythology, Folklore and Development 1500 B.C.–A.D. 1500 (Bombay, Allied Publishers, 1977)

FOREWORD

I am glad to introduce the book 'Hindu Gods and Goddesses.' I hope this book will satisfy a long-felt need for a suitable work on this subject.

What is called 'Hinduism' in the present day could not be destroyed as no invader or foreigner or practising Hindu could explore Hinduism in depth. Its roots are embedded in mysterious sources. Its branches have invaded space. Hinduism is all-pervasive, all-inclusive and penetrating into the depths.

Hinduism is supposed to be 'apauruṣeya', i.e., of impersonal origin and therefore it is devoid of errors of instrument and cognition. Even if the three Prasthānas (Authorities) namely, the Upaniṣads, the *Brahmasūtras* and the *Bhagavadgītā* did not exist, that could have hardly done any harm to Hinduism.

Even so are the gods of Hinduism. They are eternal, undecaying and undying. Some gods are prominent in the Vedas and some in later Vedic literature, Itihāsas and Purāṇās. The Vedic dictum 'Truth is one. Sages call It by different names' set the tune in the orchestra of Hinduism. This idea disproves the notion that Hinduism is polytheistic.

The Greeks had many gods and goddesses in their pantheon. They would take sides in battles or wars, hating or loving some human being. Other ancient religions and mysteries had their own gods and goddesses. In Hinduism the gods and goddesses do not take sides prominently. We may ask, 'What is the need to have so many gods in religion? Are they personifications of nature or conceptual symbols?' According to some scholars gods represent forces of nature. Agni represents fire, Vāyu the wind, Indra the thunderbolt, Soma the god of plants and liquor and so on. Here we find one tendency in the prayers of Vedic Āryans. When Varuṇa or Indra is glorified, that particular god has all the attributes of the Highest. This view also disproves the multiplicity of gods.

Hinduism has not turned its back on Vedic beliefs. On the contrary it is a continuation of Vedic tradition. Veda in its embryonic state had all the characteristics which developed in course of time. It has already been stated that each god was praised as the Highest. Naturally there was no absolute sovereign but still some gods permanently occupied a lasting place. For instance, Indra is a great warrior who drove back darkness, killed the demon Vṛtra and protected the votaries.

Towards the end of Vedic age, i.e., towards the end of 5th century B.C., there appeared the Upaniṣads. Without giving up the Vedic modes of thought, the texts revealed a sort of philosophico-gnosticism which established the relation between Ātman and Brahman. Towards the end of the Upaniṣadic period, popular Hinduism comes out in bold relief. Here we see a religion fighting against some tendencies, open to some tendencies and making the Upaniṣadic ideas more popular.

In *Bṛhadāraṇyaka Upaniṣad* we find Vidagdha Śākalya questioning Yājñavalkya thus: 'How many gods are there?' He answered in accord with the *Nivid*: 'Three hundred and three, and Three thousand and three.' By a process of regress the gods are reduced to one, the unitary Brahman. The Anglo-saxon word 'God' hardly gives the sense of the Sanskrit term 'Deva'. While God is pantheistic in Western poetry and mysticism, there is a tendency for transcedentalism in Hinduism. Nevertheless though one Godhead is emphasized, again and again a sort of trinity is recognised in Brahmā, Viṣṇu and Śiva. While Brahmā is the principle of creation, Viṣṇu preserves and Śiva destroys. Among the Vedic gods Viṣṇu and Śiva have survived, and Hinduism without Viṣṇu and Śiva is nothing. Ultimately by a series of developments Viṣṇu and Śiva are identified with the Brahman of the Upaniṣads.

There is a remarkable passage in the *Bṛhadāraṇyaka Upaniṣad*: 'The gods are fond of the cryptic, as it were, and dislike the evident' (parokṣapriyā iva hi devāḥ pratyakṣa-dviṣaḥ). Many a scholar has overlooked this esoteric sentence. The meaning is, we are not to take every sentence in an etymological sense. The names of the gods, their raiment, their instruments have got symbolic and psycho-logical significance. For instance, the Astrabhūṣana-adhyāya of *Viṣṇupurāṇa* (1.22) is a great authority on the subject. The ornaments and weapons which adorn the body of the Divine figure, symbolically represent the principles of the universe. It is thus: the living principle is in the form of Kaustubha, Prakṛti Śrīvatsa, Mahat the club, Sāttvika-ahaṅkāra the conch, Tāmasa ahaṅkāra the bow, knowledge the sword, ignorance its sheath, the mind the discus, sense and motor organs the arrows, and the subtle and gross elements the garland. Similarly we have to understand the Vedic language and the subsequent literature symbologically.

A superficial student of Hinduism sees in our religious literature much chaos and irrational practices which border on superstition. A student of Hinduism must possess a spirit of charity, dispassion and tolerance. Far from being an intellectual game, Sādhanā and philosophy are spiritual experiences. In Hinduism symbology and truth, esoteric and exoteric, Sādhanā and philosophy, psychology and ethics fascinate us.

A study of the Hindu gods is as fascinating as it is difficult. It is fascinating because of its exciting variety. It is difficult since it is symbolic. Swami Harshananda who has already written many books in English and Kannada, has handled this subject with a fair degree of care and skill. Special mention may be made of his treatment of the topics of Samudramathana and Gaṇapati.

We hope that the present work will prove to be a valuable addition to the literature on the Gods of Hinduism.

Swami Adidevananda

PREFACE

(to the second edition)

All the 2000 copies of the first edition have been exhausted within eleven months. Obviously the book has fulfilled a great need of the educated Hindus who have had little opportunity to know their gods better.

This edition is practically a reprint. Most of the drawings have been replaced by more elegant ones. Typographical errors have been minimised to the best possible extent.

We are grateful to Sri K. Balasundara Gupta for having prepared a detailed index and to Sri M.T.V. Acharya of Bangalore for supplying most of the line drawings at short notice as also to Sri B. Ramappa of Poornima Printers, Bangalore, who has done a magnificent job in printing the cover page. Our thanks to Sri R. Narasimha, who has done a fine job of printing, like last time.

The first edition could be priced low because of the generous help received from Sriyuths H.S. Subba Setty and H.S. Parthasarathy of Sakalaspur, Hassan District.

With the price index rising steeply and frequently, the price of the book has now been reluctantly raised. We hope the readers will bear with the publishers.

Date: 27-9-1982
MYSORE

Swami Harshananda

PREFACE

The peculiar characteristic of Hinduism is that it does not easily lend itself to be fitted into any rigid pattern or framework. Unlike the other great religions of the world, it does not have one founder, one scripture, or even one way of life. It is precisely due to this reason that it is sometimes dubbed, not as a religion, but only as a way of life or just a culture.

The truth, however, is otherwise. To know it, to understand it, and to appreciate it, one has to turn to the appellation by which it designates itself viz., Sanātana Dharma. Dharma in the primary sense means the Godhead that supports (dhṛ=to support) the entire creation. In the secondary sense it signifies any path that leads to it. 'Sanātana' means what is 'eternal' and 'ancient'.—Hence 'Sanātana Dharma' simply means the path of spiritual discipline, that is very ancient (Sanātana, ancient) and which when sincerely followed will invariably, (Sanātana, eternal) lead to that Godhead.

This eternal and ancient spiritual path is being revealed to different peoples of the earth in different periods of their history in different ways. Maybe, the prophets through whom it is revealed are different. Maybe, the mode of worship recommended is different. Maybe, the gods are given different names. But, the core of the teaching given by all the religions and the content of spiritual experience obtained, are identical.

Anyone who has had such experience, will be eager to teach the techniques to worthy students without dogmatising about it. As Śrī Rāmakṛṣṇa says, there can be as many spiritual paths as there are spiritual aspirants. Extending this further, we can accept as its corollary that there can be as many gods as there are devotees. As long as the central fact, viz., that these gods are the doorways leading to the one Godhead, is not forgotten, polytheism, pantheism, henotheism or 'any-theism' is acceptable. The bewildering variety of the Hindu gods should be viewed from this angle. It may be interesting to quote here from Alain Danielou's foreword to his book *Hindu Polytheism*: '....Many of the civilized nations of today are just as primitive in their beliefs and in the picture of the "god" who guides their wars and approves of their social habits and prejudices as are the most primitive tribes of India. To them the message of Hindu polytheism can be one of tolerance and understanding.'

An unbiased, if not reverent, study of the Hindu gods and goddesses can convince anyone of the rich symbology they represent. Contemplating on them with a proper understanding of their symbolical significance will help us to be raised to more profound levels of spiritual experience. Hence this humble attempt at unravelling the symbolism.

The subject matter is abstruse and literature meagre. Hence it has often been an uphill task to bring out sensible and acceptable interpretation from a medley of information available on it. How far this attempt has succeeded is left to the reader to judge.

I am grateful to Revered Swami Adidevanandaji Maharaj for blessing this work with a nice foreword. My grateful thanks are due to Swami Achalananadaji, Prof. H.G. Suryanarayana Rao and Prof.S. Srinivasachar who have gone thorough the entire manuscript, offering useful suggestions. I am indebted to Sri R. Narasimha for the personal interest taken in the printing and get-up of the book in his press.

Swami Harshananda

1
INTRODUCTION

The gods of Hinduism have successfully created enough confusion in the minds of the followers of alien faiths who have chanced to come across them. Even more successfully have they created enough conflicts among the Hindus themselves! It is ignorance that causes confusion and creates conflicts. Hence, discovering this ignorance and dispelling it should automatically lead to clearing the confusions and resolving the conflicts.

There is the story of the atheist who vehemently preached throughout his life that neither God nor soul existed, praying at the last moment of his life thus: 'O God, if there is a God, save my soul, if there is one!' This story may sound funny, but, nevertheless, it poignantly reveals man's psychological necessity for God.

Belief in God has sustained mankind for millennia. Faith in and adoration of gods and goddesses has fulfilled a practical necessity in the lives of millions of the ordinary Hindus. It is naive to suggest that the Hindus did not or could not conceive of one God, the Supreme. Philosophical thinking in Hinduism has risen to sublime heights in the Upaniṣads, the *Bhagavad Gītā* and the *Brahma Sūtras*. However, these great works, and the thinkers following in their footsteps, recognized the limitation of the average human mind and its emotional needs. That is why they wisely provided for various kinds of Upāsanas (meditations and modes of worship) to suit the different tastes and needs of the votaries.

2

THE CONCEPT OF GOD IN HINDUISM

Before proceeding further, it is worthwhile, even necessary, to know something about the concept of God in Hinduism. It is true that Hinduism does not depend upon a single scripture as the other religions of the world do. However the entire body of its philosophical literature accepts the Upaniṣads and the *Bhagavad Gītā* as authoritative and does not go against them. Hence any concept of God based on these books is welcome to practically all sections of Hinduism.

While deriving the concept of God, it is but natural for man to start from the world in which he lives and moves. So, the God of Hinduism, when looked at from this angle, is the Creator. However, He creates the entire world, not out of nothing which is illogical, but out of Himself. After creation, He sustains it with His power, rules over it like an all-powerful emperor, meting out justice, as reward and punishment, in accordance with the deeds of the individual beings. At the end of one cycle of creation—Hinduism advocates the cyclic theory of creation—He withdraws the entire world order into Himself.

The Hindu scriptures wax eloquent while describing the qualities of God. He is all-knowing and all-powerful.

He is the very personification of justice, love and beauty. In fact, He is the personification of all the blessed qualities that man can ever conceive of. He is ever ready to shower His grace, mercy and blessings on His creation. Really speaking, the very purpose of His creating this world is to shower His blessings on the creatures, to lead them gradually from less perfect states to more perfect ones. He is easily pleased by the prayers and supplication of His devotees. However His response to these prayers is guided by the principle, that it should not be in conflict with the cosmic law concerning the general welfare of the world, and the law of Karma concerning the welfare of the particular individual.

The Hindu concept of God has two special features. Depending upon the needs and tastes of his votaries, He can appear to them in any form they like to worship, and respond through that form. He can also incarnate Himself amongst human beings in order to lead them to His own kingdom. And this incarnating is a continuing process, taking place whenever and wherever He deems it necessary.

Then, there is the other aspect of God, as the Absolute. 'Brahman' is the name usually given to this aspect. It means what is infinitely big. It is the Infinite itself. It transcends everything that is created. Yet, it is immanent too, immanent in all that is created. It is so unlike anything we know that it defies all description. It has been stated that the only way by which it can be predicated, is the negative way: 'Not this! Not this!'

In its own essential nature, it is defined as 'Sat-cit-ānanda,' 'Existence-consciousness-bliss'. It is the basis or substratum of all existence, consciousness and joy.

Metaphysics points towards Brahman, the Absolute. A thinking mind and a feeling heart—that is what a human being is—can accept only God, the Creator and the Ruler (Īśvara), since the world is very much a reality to it. The correlation between the Brahman and this Īśvara, though instinctively felt by the feeling heart, will ever remain an enigma to the thinking mind! Could this be due to the mysterious power of Māyā?

3

A GENERAL NOTE ON THE GODS OF HINDUISM

The polytheism of the Hindus, though apparent, has remained a mysterious riddle. It will continue to remain so until it is viewed in the right perspective.

There are three aspects to this polytheism. The three main cult deities—the Trinity consisting of Brahmā, Viṣṇu and Śiva—along with their consorts, form the first aspect. Here all the cult deities are considered to be different facets of God, the Supreme (Īśvara). The minor deities like Gaṇeśa and Kumāra, form the second aspect. Though these deities also are sometimes described as the facets of God the Supreme, their position is usually inferior to that of the Trinity. They represent limited manifestations of the Supreme God. The Lokapālas (protectors of the world), also called as Dikpālas (protectors of the cardinal directions) like Indra, Varuṇa, Agni and others, comprise the third aspect. They are actually offices of power in the cosmic scheme of creation and human beings who have acquired extraordinary religious merit necessary for getting those places, will occupy them in each cycle of creation. Then there are any number of village deities and demigods who can be regarded either as very limited manifestations of the Supreme God or as forces of nature deified or as human beings who by virtue of some special merit and power are elevated to godhood in course of time, after their death.

The statement of Lord Śrī Kṛṣṇa in the *Bhagavad Gītā* (4.11; 7.21) that He, the Supreme Lord, will respond to the devotees in whichever form they worship Him and in whichever way they approach Him, can form the philosophical basis, typical to Hinduism, for this polytheism. So God can be all things to all men, and human beings can supplicate Him for anything—from the sublime to the ridiculous!

However, the Vedic gods form a class by themselves and so need separate treatment.

4
THE VEDIC GODS

The *Ṛgveda Saṁhitā* forms the basic scripture of Hinduism and tradition accords it the highest place. This great book is full of hymns, Sūktas as they are called, which attain supreme heights of poetical beauty and philosophical acumen, a rare combination indeed!

A major part of this work is devoted to prayers to gods like Indra, Agni, Varuṇa and others. These Vedic gods are usually enumerated as thirty three: eight Vasus, eleven Rudras, twelve Ādityas, Indra and Prajāpati. These gods are assigned to the three regions of the earth (Pṛthvī), the heavens (Dyaus) and the intermediary space, (Antarikṣa). Apart from these gods, we also find many inanimate objects like grinding stone, qualities like faith, emotions like anger, aspects of nature like dawn, deified and described. There are several female deities also, though they are not as prominent as the male deities.

Who are these gods? Are they different aspects of the One Supreme God? Or, are they different deities competing and conflicting with one another like the Greek gods? Or, are they just animals and totems masquerading as gods?! Since the main purpose of this small book is to acquaint the average reader with a general idea of gods and goddesses in Hinduism, we cannot embark upon a research into this aspect of the question. Suffice it to say that the famous statement in the *Ṛgveda* itself viz., 'ekam sat viprāḥ bahudhā vadanti,' 'Truth is One; sages call It by various names' (1.164.46) sets the tone for the philosophy of the Vedas which is amplified later on by the Upaniṣads. Hence, though these deities appear to be different and independent, they are really facets of the same Brahman, the Supreme God.

Let us now consider briefly the more important of these deities. For the sake of convenience they are arranged and dealt with in alphabetical order:

Ādityas: The Ādityas represent a group of deities. They are six in the *Ṛgveda*, eight in most of the Brāhmaṇas, but become twelve in the *Śatapatha Brāhmaṇa*. In the later mythological literate, they are always twelve.

The Ādityas can be described as the personifications of laws that rule the universe and the human society. They regulate the relationships of human beings among themselves and with the forces of nature.

Āditya is one of the names of the sun. Hence the Ādityas can be taken as the imperishable eternal beings, the gods of light, by whom all manner of luminous life is manifested and sustained in this universe.

The twelve Ādityas are: Mitra (the friend), Varuṇa (one who encompasses and binds), Aryaman (the destroyer of foes), Dakṣa (the skilful), Bhaga (the giver), Aṁśa (the liberal), Tvaṣṭṛ (the shaper), Savitṛ (the vivifier), Pūṣan (the nourisher), Śakra (the mighty), Vivasvat (the resplendent) and Viṣṇu (the pervader).

Sometimes, the twelve Ādityas are linked with the twelve aspects of the sun spread over the twelve months and hence described as the twelve spokes of the wheel of time.

Agni: Since the religion of the *Ṛgveda* was mainly sacrificial, Agni, the god of fire, naturally got the pride of place. A maximum number of hymns are devoted to describing and praising Agni. He is often eulogised as the Supreme God, the creator, the sustainer, the all-pervading cosmic spirit. All other gods are his different manifestations. He manifests himself as fire (Agni) on this earth (Pṛthvī), as lightning or air (Indra or Vāyu) in the sky (Antarikṣa) and as the sun (Sūrya) in the heavens (Dyuloka). He acts as a mediator between men and gods by carrying the offerings of men to gods. He is all-knowing and all-powerful. He is all-merciful too. Though an immortal, he lives among the mortals, in every house. He protects them by dispelling their difficulties and giving them whatever they pray for. Without him, the world can never sustain itself.

In later literature, Agni is described as the lord presiding over the southeast quarter.

The image of Agni in temples, represents him as an old man with a red body. He has two heads, a big belly and six eyes, seven arms in which he holds objects like the spoon, ladle, fan etc., seven tongues, four horns and three legs. He has braided hair, wears red garment as also the Yajñopavīta (the sacred thread). He is attended on either side by his two consorts, Svāhā and Svadhā. The smoke is his banner and ram, his vehicle. Obviously, this is an anthropomorphic representation of the sacrificial fire.

Aśvins: These are twin deities, always described or praised together. What exactly they represent, is a moot point. While some say that they represent the earth and the sky, there are others who opine that they stand for night and day or the moon and the sun. That they were once kings who acquired extraordinary merit, and were elevated to the position of gods, is another guess that is also hazarded sometimes.

They represent the semidarkness before dawn. They pervade this world with moisture and light. Described as eternally young and handsome, they are the youngest of the gods. However, their chief characteristic is that

Fig. 1. Agni

they are constantly striving to do good to others. They are expert physicians and surgeons and know the arts of healing, rejuvenation, and even plastic surgery! Being supplicated, they can grant boons like children, food, wealth, health and protection from enemies. Hence one should never fail to invoke them during sacrifices.

Indra: Indra, undoubtedly, is the chief deity in the *Ṛgveda*. Almost a quarter of its hymns, is devoted to praising him. He is the most important deity in the sky. Armed with the thunderbolt (Vajrāyudha) and riding in a chariot whose speed exceeds that of the mind, he travels everywhere.

His valour is awe-inspiring. His exploits are many. He killed the demon Vṛtra and released the waters imprisoned by him. He clipped the wings of the mighty mountains and made them behave. He recovered the cows of the gods that had been abducted by the demons. He is fond of Soma-drink. Being a war-lord, he became a symbol of the royal power. Hence warriors worshipped him before going to the battle-field.

Indra has often been equated with the Supreme God. His love and affection for his devotees has been eulogized. Scholars opine that Indra may just represent the natural phenomenon of rain being released from the dark clouds as a result of being "bombarded by lightning and thunder"!

Indra's prestige gradually declined and he was relegated to a secondary place by the Purāṇas, retaining however, his place as the king of gods.

Fig. 2. Indra

In some of the temple sculptures, Indra is depicted in a human form with four arms, riding the celestial elephant Airāvata.

Rudra and Rudras: Rudra is the god who howls or roars. He is terrible. He is tall and well-built. He has a long braided hair. His body is brilliant and its colour merges with the colour of the gold ornaments he wears. He wields the thunderbolt, bow and arrow. He is the god of storms. Though he looks fierce and is armed with terrible weapons, he is always benevolent and merciful to humanity. He is the protector, the kind and loving father, protecting humanity against its enemies. He is extraordinarily intelligent and wise. He is an excellent physician. He has thousands of medicines with him which can cure all the diseases of humanity.

Rudra has sometimes been identified with Agni. He has also been described as the father of the Maruts, another class of Vedic deities. Some of the names like Śiva, Kapardin, Mahādeva and so on, which have been used in the later mythological literature as epithets of Śiva have been used in the *Ṛgveda* also.

It is very difficult to say exactly which aspects of nature Rudra represents.

Sometimes a group of minor deities called the Rudras is also mentioned. They are eleven in number. They are actually the principles of life (Prāṇas), the ten vital breaths and the mind.

Rudras are also mentioned as eight in number and the eight names—Bhava, Śarva, Īśāna, Paśupati, Bhīma, Ugra, Mahādeva along with Rudra—represent the eight aspects of Rudra-Śiva in later literature.

Soma: Soma, also called as Indu or Soma-Pavamāna, is one of the most important deities in the *Ṛgveda*. The entire ninth Maṇḍala is devoted to his praise. He is the presiding deity of the Soma creeper whose juice is often used in sacrifices as offering and also drink. He is sometimes praised as the Supreme God. He cures the mortals of their diseases, gives them joy and leads them to immortal blissful worlds. It was because of the power he bestowed that Indra was able to do wonderful deeds and slay the demon Vṛtra. He rules over the mind and activates speech. Hence he is sometimes described as Vācaspati, 'lord of speech'. It is he who makes ordinary mortals Ṛṣis, wise sages. He creates the worlds, rules over mountains and rivers.

The name Soma has been used in the *Ṛgveda* for the deity that animates the Soma creeper, the juice of the creeper itself, as also the moon. In later literature, Some has been practically identified with the moon itself. Scholars opine that the deity Homa of the *Zend-Avesta* is this Soma itself.

Sūrya: Sūrya or the sun, often identified with Āditya, Savitṛ and Pūṣan, is another important Vedic deity. He is extremely brilliant and rides in an exquisitely beautiful chariot drawn by seven horses. He is compared to a bird that flies in the sky and is described as the jewel of the sky. He gives light, produces day and night, gives power and strength to the living beings, makes them active and destroys their laziness and disease.

Savitṛ is the aspect of the sun before sunrise. He is golden all over. He establishes people in their respective places. He gives life and energy and guides people in the right path.

Fig. 3. Sūrya

The famous Gāyatrī Mantra is dedicated to this Savitṛ.

The nourishing and life-supporting aspect of the sun is personified and praised as Pūṣan. He is exceedingly beautiful. He destroys the evil ones with the discus he wears. He looks upon all with an equal eye. He is extremely generous and ever ready to protect.

Varuṇa: Varuṇa 'the one who econompasses the whole world,' is one of the oldest Vedic deities. May be he

Fig. 4. Varuṇa

is the personification of the sky; but he is also associated with clouds and water, rivers and ocean. He is sometimes clubbed with Mitra and praised (Mitrāvaruṇa).

Varuṇa is the king of the universe and lives in the highest world. His knowledge and power are unlimited. He has thousand eyes and oversees the whole world. Hence he is the lord of the moral law. He punishes those who transgress this law but forgives them out of compassion if they repent and pray. By activating Vāyu, the lord of the wind, he sustains life by giving rain and crops.

Though Varuṇa was the chief deity in the beginning, he seems to have yielded his place later on to Indra and Prajāpati.

In the subsequent mythological literature Varuṇa is described as the presiding deity of the western quarter and as the lord of oceans, water and aquatic animals. In some of the temples he is depicted as riding on a crocodile. In two of his four arms he holds the serpent and the noose (pāśa). Sometimes he is pictured as riding in a chariot drawn by seven swans and holding the lotus, the noose, the conch and a vessel of gems in the four hands. There is an umbrella over his head.

Vasus: Vasus are a class of deities, eight in number, chiefly known as attendants of Indra. The word Vasu is derived from 'vas' ('to dwell,' 'to cause to dwell,' 'to shine') and hence Vasus are deities representing all spheres of extension or space, and height. They were perhaps personifications of nature and natural phenomena.

The eight Vasus are: Dharā (the earth), Anala (the fire), Ap (the waters), Anila, (the wind), Dhruva (the polestar), Soma (the moon), Prabhāsa (the dawn) and Pratyūṣa, (the light).

Vāyu: Vāyu is the god of, or personification of, wind, air or lifebreath (Prāṇa). As the lord of the sky (Antarikṣa) he shares his power with Indra. He rides in a chariot drawn by two, ninety-nine, hundred or even thousand horses, (the number perhaps, depends upon his wish to produce an ordinary wind current or a storm or a cyclone!) His chariot announces his arrival with terrific roars. However, he himself is invisible. Like Indra he is also fond of the Soma juice. It is he who is the basis of all life here. Inside our bodies he works as the five vital airs (Pañcaprāṇa). Like Rudra, he is also a physician and can effect wonderful cures.

In mythology he is the ruler of the north-western quarter. He is described as blue in colour and as holding a fan and a flag in two hands, the other two hands showing the Abhaya and Varada Mudrās (indicating protection and granting of gifts).

Viṣṇu: It is rather strange that Viṣṇu (i.e., 'one who pervades'), the Supreme deity of the Vaiṣṇava tradition, the second of the Trinity and highly popular deity of later Hinduism, finds a secondary place in the *Ṛgveda*. He is a friend of Indra. He is a solar deity, an aspect of sun when he envelops the whole universe with his rays. The words Urugāya and Trivikrama, meaning one who has great strides or who covers the universe in three steps signify the sun as he crosses the sky in the three times of the day, viz., dawn, day and dusk. His abode has been highly eulogised. He is described as the personification of time. He is an eternal youth and extremely handsome. The sun is sometimes described as his discus. He is the creator and protector of the worlds. There is none equal to or superior to him. He is extremely kind and generous. He is easily pleased by the offerings made at the sacrifice also.

Viśvedevas: Literally the word means 'all the gods.' Perhaps, all the gods left over without being specifically mentioned in prayers, are meant to be included under this word. But they gradually seem to evolve as a specific group like the Ādityas or the Maruts. These deities are the protectors of Ṛta, the moral law. They destroy the enemies of their devotees, protect the good, give auspicious abodes and control like kings. They are ever young and handsome. They are easily pleased by devoted obeisance.

Later mythology describes them usually as ten in number: Vasu (dwelling place), Satya (truth), Kratu (will), Dakṣa (skill), Kāla (time), Kāma (desire), Dhṛti (forbearance), Kuru (the ancestor of the Kurus), Purūravas (a being dwelling in the atmosphere), Mādravas (cry of joy). These deities are said to be fond of funeral offerings.

Yama: Yama is one who restrains, who curbs, who controls. He was the first of men to die and to depart to the celestial world. He is the god of the dead and so the spirits of the departed dwell with him. He has two very fierce dogs, with four eyes and wide nostrils, which guard the path of the departed souls leading to Yama's kingdom.

In the mythological literature he is described as the god of death and the judge, Dharmarāja, meting out rewards and punishments to the souls of the dead brought to him. In this he is ably assisted by Citragupta, the recorder.

He is the ruler of the southern quarter, is green in colour, wears red garments, has a mighty mace and noose, and rides a he-buffalo.

5
THE TRINITY

Broadly speaking, Hindus can be divided into three main groups: Saivas or those who worship Śiva, Śāktas or those who worship Śakti (consort of Śiva), and Vaiṣṇavas or those who worship Viṣṇu. However, popular Hindu theology, which has its roots in the ancient scriptures, adds another important deity, Brahmā. The three—Brahmā, Viṣṇu and Śiva—together form the Hindu Trinity.

Brahmā creates the world, Viṣṇu sustains it and Śiva destroys it. This process of creation (sṛṣṭi), preservation (sthiti) and destruction (pralaya) perpetually continues in that cyclic order.

If the world were a myth as some extreme forms of Advaita Vedānta philosophy aver, there would have been no theology and hence no theological problems. But the world being a fact of our day-to-day experience, cannot be explained away or wished away! Once we accept it as real—whatever may be the degree of reality we ascribe to it—the theological questions of creations and creator will have to be squarely faced and answered. This is what the various Hindu scriptures have attempted.

Three types of tendencies or characteristics seem to accrue to every created object. These have been technically designated as Guṇas: Sattvaguṇa, Rajoguṇa and Tamoguṇa. These three Guṇas in their purest form, are fundamental entities, the permutation and combination of which produce this world of phenomena. Of these, the Sattvaguṇa makes for light and lightness, goodness and purity, knowledge and wisdom. It can be likened to the centripetal force. Tamoguṇa, which is the antithesis of Sattvaguṇa, is responsible for all that is dark and heavy, evil and impure, ignorant and deluded. It is the centrifugal force as it were. It is the business of Rajoguṇa to maintain a delicate balance between these two opposing forces. Hence it has got to be in a state of constant internal tension and activity. This restless activity is its chief characteristic and it manifests itself as passion and ambition in the psychological world.

The three deities of the Trinity, correspond to the three Guṇas in the cosmic play of creation, preservation and destruction. Viṣṇu represents Sattva, the power of existence and preservation. Śiva represents Tamas, the power of annihilation. Brahmā stands in between these two and represents Rajas. He symbolises the possibility of existence resulting from the union of opposites.

Brahmā

Thus Brahmā is the source, the seed, of all that is. He is, as his very name indicates, boundless immensity, from which space, time and causation originate, names and

Fig. 5. Brahmā

forms spring up. Philosophically, he is the first stage of manifestation of the notion of individual existence (Ahaṅkāra). Theologically, he is the uncreated creator (Svayambhū), the self-born first Person.

He has several designations which are as instructive as they are interesting. From the cosmological point of view he is the Golden Embryo (Hiraṇyagarbha), the ball of fire, from which the universe develops. Since all created beings are his progency, he is Prajāpati, the lord of progeny, as also Pitāmaha, the patriarch. He is Vidhi, the ordinator, and Lokeśa, the master of the worlds, as well as Dhātṛ, the sustainer. He is also Viśvakarmā, the architect of the world.

Hindu mythological literature describes Brahmā as having sprung from the lotus orginating from the navel of Viṣṇu. Hence he is called Nābhija (navel-born), Kañja (water-born) and so on.

Curiously enough, the name Nārāyaṇa ('one who dwells in the causal waters' or 'the abode of man') has been applied to him first and only later to Viṣṇu.

Brahmā, the creator, and Sarasvatī, his consort, are the subject of several tales in our mythological literature. They can be summaraised briefly thus:

(1) Brahmā was born out of the golden egg produced in the boundless causal waters. His consort Vāc or Sarasvatī was manifested out of him. From their union were born all the creatures of the world.

(2) Brahmā represents the Vedas and Sarasvatī their spirit and meaning. Hence, all knowledge, sacred and secular, has proceeded from them.

(3) Once Brahmā became the boar and raised the earth from beneath the waters and created the world, the sages and Prajāpatis. (This story was later transferred to Viṣṇu).

(4) The forms of tortoise and fish (later considered as Avatāras of Viṣṇu) have been attributed to Brahmā also.

(5) The great sages Marīcī, Atri, Aṅgiras and others are his 'mind-born' children. Manu, the Adam of the Āryan race, is his great-grandson.

(6) He is easily pleased by austerities and bestows boons on the supplicants, be they gods, demons or men.

(7) He is the inventor of the theatrical art. Music, dance and stagecraft were revealed by him.

(8) He was the chief priest who performed the marriage of Śiva with Pārvatī.

In spite of the fact that Brahmā is God the Supreme in the creative aspect and is an equally important member of the Hindu Trinity, it is strange that there are no temples dedicated exclusively to him, the one at Puṣkar being the solitary exception. Notwithstanding the crude reasons given in some of the Purāṇas for this loss of Brahmā's prestige, some scholars opine* that the Brahmā cult was predominant in the pre-Vedic Hinduism and was superseded or suppressed by the later Śiva-Viṣṇu cults.

In fact, the evolution of the Śakti concept—each of the gods Śiva and Viṣṇu having his Śakti or Power as his consort—and the explanation that creation proceeds out of

---

* See *The Cult of Brahmā*, by Tārāpāda Bhattācārya, pp. 88–89.

the combination of the god and his Śakti, has made Brahmā superfluous.

The icon of Brahmā has four heads facing the four quarters; and they represent the four Vedas, the four Yugas (epochs of time), and the four Varṇas (divisions of society based on nature, nurture and vocation). Usually, the faces have beards and the eyes are closed in meditation. There are four arms holding different objects and in different poses. The arms represent the four quarters. The objects usually shown are: Akṣamālā (rosary), Kūrca (a brush of Kuśa grass), Sruk (ladle), Sruva (spoon), Kamaṇḍalu (water pot) and Pustaka (book). The combination and arrangement vary from image to image. The rosary represents time, and the water pot, the causal waters, from which all creation has sprung. So, Brahmā controls time as well as the principle of causation. The Kuśa grass, the ladle and the spoon being sacrificial implements, represent the system of sacrifices which is the means to be adopted by the various creatures to sustain one another. The book represents knowledge, sacred and secular. He is the giver of all knowledge—arts, sciences and wisdom.

The poses of the hand (Mudrās) are Abhaya (assuring protection) and Varada (granting boons).

The icon may be either in standing posture (standing on a lotus) or in sitting posture (sitting on a Haṁsa or swan). Haṁsa, his vehicle, stands for discrimination and wisdom.

Sometimes, Brahmā is shown as riding in a chariot drawn by seven swans, standing for the seven worlds.

In temples exclusively dedicated to Brahmā, his aspect as Viśvakarmā (the architect of the universe) is adopted. In this form he is shown as having four heads, four arms holding the rosary, the book, the Kuśa grass and the water pot, and riding on his swan.

Every temple, be it of Śiva, or Viṣṇu, must have a niche in the northern wall for Brahmā, and his image must receive worship every day since he is an important Parivāradevatā (attendant of the Chief-deity).

6

THE TRINITY (Continued)

Viṣṇu

Viṣṇu, also known as Mahāviṣṇu, is the second deity of the Hindu Trinity. He represents Sattvaguṇa and is the centripetal force as it were, responsible for sustenance, protection and maintenance of the created universe.

Etymologically speaking, the word 'Viṣṇu' means 'one who pervades, one who has entered into everything.' So he is the transcendent as well the immanent reality of the universe. He is the inner cause and power by which things exist.

Another name of Viṣṇu which is extremely common and popular is Nārāyaṇa. The word means:

(a) One who has made the causal waters his abode;

(b) One who is the abode of all human beings;

(c) One who has made the hearts of human beings his abode;

(d) One who is the final goal of all human beings.

Fig. 6. Viṣṇu

The first interpretation has given rise to a description of Nārāyaṇa which is common and popular, as follows:

After the destruction of the universe of the previous cycle and before the creation of the next, Nārāyaṇa, the Supreme God, falls asleep on his bed of the great serpent Śeṣa (also called Ananta), which is floating on the waters of the ocean Kṣīramudra ('ocean of milk'). One of his legs is resting on the lap of his consort Lakṣmī, who is gently pressing it. When he is dreaming as it were, of the next creation, a lotus springs forth from his navel along with god Brahmā seated on it. After waking up, he instructs Brahmā to proceed with the act of creation.

This is a highly allegorical picture. The ocean represents causal waters from which all life springs a concept not uncommonly found in other religions also. Or, since it is Kṣīrasamudra, the ocean of milk, it stands for the purest form of Prakṛti or nature in its undifferentiated state, whiteness indicating this purity.

Out of the several equivalents of the word Āpas (=water), is the word Amṛta (=nectar, signifying bliss also). Hence we can say that the Lord Nārāyaṇa is floating on the ocean of bliss, which is as it should be.

The serpent Śeṣa or Ananta is said to have a thousand heads and is supporting the worlds on its hoods. Ananta, which literally means the 'endless' or 'infinite' actually stands for cosmic time which is infinite or endless. Created worlds come into being in time and are sustained in time. This is the meaning of the thousand hoods supporting the worlds. The thousand hoods, simply indicate the innumerable divisions of time.

The concept of the thousand hoods supporting the worlds can also lead to the interpretation that the serpent represents the cosmic space, in which everything exists.

The word Śeṣa is also significant. It actually means 'the remainder', 'what is left over at the end'. Since creation cannot proceed out of nothing, it is to be assumed that 'something' is 'left over' (śeṣa) from the previous creation, which forms the seed as it were, for the next. So, Śeṣa represents the totality of the Jīvas or individual souls in their subtle form, left over from the previous cycle and needing more opportunities for regeneration.

Serpent can also represent Kāma or desire which is always left over (śeṣa), even after acquisition and enjoyment of the desired object. This goes on until Mokṣa or final liberation. Hence, in a cosmic sense, it can stand for the desire of the Lord to proceed with the next cycle of creation after rest!

Viṣṇu is always described as Nīlameghaśyāma, of a dark blue hue like that of the rain-bearing cloud. Since the infinite empty space appears as deep blue in colour, it is but proper that Viṣṇu the all-pervading cosmic power, be depicted as blue in colour.

The commonest form of the Viṣṇu icon has one face, four arms holding Śaṅkha (conch), Cakra (discus), Gadā (mace), Padma (lotus) and wears a necklace with the famous gem Kaustubha dangling on the lock of hair Śrīvatsa, on the left chest. He is also wearing a garland (of gems, or fragrant flowers) Vaijayantī by name.

The four arms represents the four quaters, hence, absolute power of the Lord in all directions. The Śaṅkha represents the five elements like the earth, water etc., Cakra stands for the cosmic mind, Gadā indicates the cosmic intellect and the Padma points to the evolving world. Just as the lotus is born out of water and unfolds gradually in all its glory, this world also is born out of the causal waters and evolves gradually in all its splendour. Hence the lotus stands for the evolved world. This world can be created only by a combination of the five elements, the mind and the intellect. Hence the total meaning of this symbology would be that the Lord Viṣṇu is the creator and master of this world.

The curl of hair, Śrīvatsa, represents all objects of enjoyment, the products of nature. The gem Kaustubha, resting on it, stands for the enjoyer. So, this world of duality consisting of the enjoyer and the enjoyed, is like an ornament for the Lord. The garland Vaijayantī is symbolical of the subtle elements (bhūta-tanmātras).

Sometimes two more weapons, Nandaka the sword (representing wisdom) and Śārṅga the bow (representing the cosmic senses) are added to the arsenal of Lord Viṣṇu.

AVATĀRAS (INCARNATIONS) OF LORD VIṢṆU:

To ward off the extraordinary perils to which mankind is prone—maybe the visitations from the demons, maybe from the human malefactors—and to preserve the socio-ethical order, Lord Viṣṇu whose duty it is to preserve this world, often incarnates himself. Though such incarnations are popularly considered to be ten, there is no limit to their number. Nor are there any restrictions regarding the time and place of their appearance. Whenever Dharma declines and Adharma prospers He bodies Himself forth to restore the balance in the world.

In the Matsyāvatāra (Fish-incarnation), the Lord is said to have saved Manu (the progenitor of mankind) and the Saptarṣis (the seven sages, mind-born sons of Brahmā) along with their wives during the deluge. The world was repopulated through them later on.

Lord Viṣṇu incarnated himself as the Kūrma (the Tortoise) in order to support the mount Mandara which started sinking during the churning of the ocean (Samudra-mathana). The gods and the demons had jointly undertaken this adventure to get Amṛta (nectar) from the ocean.

Next in the series is the Varāhāvatāra (Boar-incarnation) in which the Lord killed the demon Hiraṇyākṣa and lifted the earth out of the flood waters in which it had been submerged. This may be a symbolic representation of the extrication of the world from the deluge of sin by the power of the Supreme Being.

When Prahlāda, the great devotee of Viṣṇu was being severely tortured by his father, the demon Hiraṇyakaśipu, (who was a non-believer in the existence of an omnipresent and omnipotent God), Narasiṁha (Man-lion) appeared, emerging out of the pillar shown by him and killed him. Being a combination of man (the best of higher creatures) and lion (the best of lower creatures) Narasiṁha represents the best of creation. Incidentally this also proves the omnipresence of God. Narasiṁha is especially the embodiment of valour which is a divine attribute and hence worshipped by rulers and warriors. His Mantra is said to be very powerful, capable of destroying enemies and exorcising evil.

Fig.7. Matsyāvatāra

Fig.8. Kūrmāvatāra

Fig.9. Varāhāvatāra

Fig.10. Narasiṁhāvatāra

Fig.11. Vāmanāvatāra

When Bali the grandson of Prahlāda conquered the three worlds, Indra was deprived of his heavenly kingdom. At the request of Aditi, the mother of Indra, Lord Viṣṇu incarnated as Vāmana (the Dwarf), a young Brāhmaṇa boy, and approached Bali who was known for his munificence, for a gift of land that could be covered by three steps. With the first and the second he covered the earth and heaven, and with the third, he pushed down Bali to the netherworld. Hence he is also known as Trivikrama, one who encompassed the world with three big steps.

This myth teaches us that since even God had to resort to the dwarf's form while begging, one who begs makes himself small! Secondly, a true Brāhmaṇa can conquer the three worlds by the power of the spirit. These five Avatāras have been referred to in the various sections of the Vedas.

The next five incarnations are in the human form.

Paraśurāma (Rāma with the battle-axe) is the sixth Avatāra. Born as the son of the sage-couple, Jamadagni and Reṇukā, he exterminated the tyrannical among the Kṣattriyas led by Kārtavīrya, who were oppressing the people. Whether this story has any historical basis and represents the struggle for supremacy between the Brāhmaṇas and Kṣattriyas, it is difficult to say.

Śrī Rāma, the next incarnation, met Paraśurāma and absorbed his power into himself. Hence the latter is sometimes considered as āveśāvatāra, an incarnation by the temporary possession of Viṣṇu's powers.

Śrī Rāma, one of the two most popular incarnations of the Lord Viṣṇu, comes next in the series. His story is too

Fig. 12. Paraśurāmāvatāra

Fig. 13. Śrī Rāmāvatāra

well-known to need any repetition. He typifies the ideal man. His story, the *Rāmāyaṇa* has now become an immortal epic. His name is known as the 'Tāraka-mantra,' the Mantra that takes one across the ocean of transmigration.

Balarāma, Rāma the strong, the elder brother of Śrī Kṛṣṇa, is the eighth incarnation. His many adventures include the slaying of the ape Dvivida and the demon Dhenuka, shaking the ramparts of Hastināvati (the capital city of the Pāṇḍavas) and dragging the river Yamunā out of its course. The story that the serpent Śeṣa issued forth from his mouth at the time of his death gives credence to the belief that he was the incarnation of Śeṣa. Some scholars, basing their conjecture on the weapon of Balarāma (the Hala or plough), opine that he was an agricultural hero raised to the status of an Avatāra in course of time.

Śrī Kṛṣṇa, the ninth incarnation of Lord Viṣṇu is, perhaps, the most popular, so much so, that he is considered Pūrṇāvatāra (the incarnation *in toto*) and all other deities are regarded as his manifestations. His story and his exploits are too numerous and too wellknown to be mentioned here. To the average Hindu, he is the supreme statesman, warrior, hero, philosopher and teacher, nay, God Himself. He is the great expounder of the 'Song Celestial,' the *Bhagavad Gītā*.

The tenth Avatāra Kalki, is yet to come. He will descend upon the earth at the end of the present age (Kali Yuga). Riding on the back of a white horse, with a drawn sword, he will destroy the enemies of Dharma and re-establish it in all its glory.

Fig. 14. Balarāmāvatāra

Fig. 15. Kṛṣṇāvatāra

Fig. 16. Buddhāvatāra

Fig. 17. Kalki-avātāra

This list of the ten Avatāras of Lord Viṣṇu is by no means the standard one accepted by all. Taking Śrī Kṛṣṇa as Viṣṇu Himself, he is not included in some lists. His place is taken over by Buddha. In some other lists, Buddha replaces Balarāma. Iconographically speaking, Buddha seems to have disappeared from such lists only after the 15th century.

Strangely enough, the purpose of the Buddha-incarnation was to mislead men of low birth and genius, who had become too proficient in the sacred lore and were a threat to the supermacy of the gods! This looks more like a joke than a serious proposition. It is obvious that the Hindus sealed the fate of Buddhism in this country by absorbing Buddha into the pantheon of the Avatāras.

Haṁsa, Sātvata, Yajña, Dattātreya, Vedavyāsa are some of the Avatāras included in other lists, keeping the total as ten only. The number, however, rises sometimes to as high as twentythree.

CATURVYŪHAS:

The Bhāgavata or the Pāñcarātra religion, which preaches the cult of Viṣṇu-Nārāyaṇa, puts forth the theory that the Supreme Lord Viṣṇu has four aspects of manifestation: (a) the Para or the supreme; (b) the Vyūha or the emanation; (c) the Vibhava or the incarnation and (d) the Arca or icon.

Para is the Supreme as He is, in all His glory. Vibhava represents the incarnations already dealt with. Arca is the descent of the Lord into the icon ceremonially installed and worshipped in the temples.

The Vyūhas or the emanations are four in number. Hence the term caturvyūhas, also called caturmūrtis. They are: Vāsudeva, Saṅkarṣaṇa, Pradyumna and Aniruddha. According to Vaiṣṇava mythologies, while Śrī Kṛṣṇa is Vāsudeva, his brother Balarāma is Saṅkarṣana. Pradyumna and Aniruddha are Kṛṣṇa's son and grandson respectively. Historically speaking, it is possible that these Yādava heroes were, in course of time, apotheosised into these Vyūhas. Symbologically, Vāsudeva represents Citta (mind-stuff), whereas Saṅkarṣana stands for Ahaṇkāra (egoity), Pradyumna for Buddhi (intellect) and Aniruddha for Manas (mind). They represent the cosmic psychological evolution.

Later on, these Vyūhas were increased to as many as twenty-four. Iconographically, all these Vyūhas are identical in appearance except for the arrangement of the four emblems—Śaṅkha, Cakra, Gadā and Padma.

The Pāñcarātra theology often adds another aspect of the manifestations, viz., the Antaryāmin (the indweller), which obviously, cannot be represented through icons.

MINOR INCARNATIONS

Hindu mythology abounds in stories of Lord Viṣṇu's Avatāras, which may be Pūrnāvatāras (full manifestations) like Śrī Kṛṣṇa, Aṁśāvatāras (partial manifestations) like Kapila or Āveśāvatāras (temporary infilling of the divine power) like Paraśurāma. A few of these may now be dealt with.

Dattātreya:

He was the son of the great sage Atri and his wife Anasūyā, one of the paragons of chastity in Hindu mythology. He was the originator of certain magical rites and the creator of the Soma plant. He was a teacher of non-Āryan people. Association with people of low birth and objects of pleasure, has made him ritually impure. But, learning and englightenment have made him so pure that nothing can ever stain him. Being the incarnation of the Trinity, he is shown as having three heads, four hands and accompanied by four dogs of different colours which represent the four Vedas.

The Dattātreya concept may be an attempt at harmonising the three cults of Brahmā, Viṣṇu and Śiva. It may also have been the medium through which non-Vedic cults were brought into the Hindu fold.

Dhanvantari:

Dhanvantari rose from the ocean, at the time of churning, holding the Amṛta-kalaśa (pot of ambrosia) in his hand. He is the originator of medical sciences. Reborn as the king of Kāśī he brought medical science to the earth.

Vedas also mention a Dhanvantari, a god associated with herbs and medicines.

He is described as a handsome person holding the pot of ambrosia and seated in front of Viṣṇu's insignias.

Hayagrīva or Hayaśīrṣa:

Yājñavalkya, the great sage, lost the *Yajurveda* as a result of his Guru's curse and performed severe penance.

Fig. 18. Hayagrīva

Sun-god, pleased by his penance, appeared before him as a deity with the horse's head and taught him the same Veda in another form. This section has come to be known as the *Vājasaneyī Saṁhitā* (Vāji=horse). The origins of the Hayagrīva Avatāra (the deity with the horse's head) are perhaps found here.

Two demons Madhu and Kaiṭabha had stolen the Vedas and hidden them under water. Lord Viṣṇu took the form of Hayagrīva, dived to the bottom of the ocean and rescued them after killing the demons.

Hayagrīva is the god of learning, akin to the goddess Sarasvatī.

He is shown in the human form, with the horse's head, possessing four or eight arms, carrying the various weapons and emblems of Viṣṇu.

Kapila:

Kapila, the son of Kardama and Devahūtī was a great sage who reduced to ashes the sixty thousand sons of the king Sagara, just by a glance. Probably this story is at the back of his being identified sometimes with Agni. He taught Sāṅkhya philosophy to his mother.

Kapila icons usually have the hair dressed up as a crown (Jaṭā-mukuṭa), a beard, four arms, two of which are in Yoga holding a pitcher and the other two holding Śaṅkha and Cakra.

Mohinī:

At the behest of the gods who had been deprived of the ambrosia by the demons during the churning of the ocean, Lord Viṣṇu appeared as Mohinī, the enchantress, who successfully duped the demons and distributed the nectar among the gods. Even Śiva is said to have been bewitched by her beauty.

The story teaches us that immortality (Amṛtatva) can be gained only by the conquest of delusion (Moha).

Mohinī is shown as a beautiful young woman wearing colourful garments, decorated with ornaments and carrying a vase of nectar in hand.

Nara-Nārāyaṇa:

After the purpose of Narasiṁha-avatāra was accomplished, Narasiṁha split himself into two, the lion part becoming the sage Nārāyaṇa and the human part the sage Nara. Nara and Nārāyaṇa then retired to Badarikāśrama for performing austerities. When Indra tried to seduce them through celestial nymphs, Nārāyaṇa produced the nymph Ūrvaśī from his thigh (ūru=thigh) who was more beautiful than all of them put together.

According to another version, these sages were sons of Dharma and Ahiṁsā. They performed severe austerities and successfully vanquished the demon Sahasrakavaca (one who has a thousand armours).

These sages were reborn later as Śrī Kṛṣṇa and Arjuna.

This story has an important lesson for us. Everyone of us is a mixture of the human and the divine elements. The anti-human and the anti-divine demon is ever attempting to seduce us with his thousand wiles. To successfully vanquish him, we need to perform Tapas or austerity.

Fig. 19. Nara-Nārāyaṇa

Nara-Nārāyaṇa is represented either as a single person or as two persons. In the former case the icon may have two or four arms carrying the Japamālā (rosary) or the usual emblems of Lord Viṣṇu. In the latter case, Nara may be shown as having two heads and two arms and wearing the deer skin. Nārāyaṇa is depicted with the usual four arms carrying the emblems Śaṅkha, Cakra, Padma and Japamālā.

Vyāsa:

Vyāsa is a cosmic entity born in every age to propagate the scriptures.

The sage Kṛṣṇa-Dvaipāyana, the son of Parāśara, is the well-known Vyāsa of this age. He got that name since he colleted all the extant Vedic hymns and divided them (vyas=to divide) into the four Vedas. He is the author of the great epic *Mahābhārata* as also all the Purāṇas (mythologies) and the *Brahmasūtras*.

In images, he is shown as of slender build, dark in complexion and with the hair dressed up as a crown. His four disciples Paila, Vaiśampāyana, Jaimini and Sumantu are also shown by his side.

Yajña:

Viṣṇu has been identified with Yajña or sacrifice in early Vedic literature. The *Bhāgavata* calls Varāhāvatāra as Yajña-varāha and identifies his limbs with the various parts of a sacrifice. In other mythological lore, he as Yajñeśa, is describes as the son of Ruci and Ākūti. The entire universe which is in a constant state of flux is like a sacrifice and the Lord responsible for this creation is looked upon as the personification of that sacrifice. Hence he is Yajña or Yajñeśvara.

His image has two heads, seven hands, three legs and four horns. The hands carry the sacrificial implements like Ājyapātra (vessel holding the ghee) Sruk, Sruva and Juhū (various kinds of spoons and ladles), apart from Śaṅkha and Cakra.

Obviously this is a symbolical representation, the various limbs representing the various items of the sacrifice. The description is rather too technical to be dealt with in a small work like this.

OTHER ASPECTS OF VIṢNU COMMONLY WORSHIPPED

Jagannātha of Puri in Orissa is a Vaiṣṇava deity which draws huge crowds, especially during the annual car festival. The image appears rather grotesque and is shaped out of a log and has prominent eyes. Once in twelve years the log-image is renewed, the log being brought every time mysteriously. The insertion of some ancient relic into the new image sanctifies it. It represents Śrī Kṛṣṇa with similar images representing Balarāma and Subhadrā (Kṛṣṇa's sister).

Pāṅduraṇga Viṭṭhala commonly known as Viṭṭhala or Viṭhoba is the deity of the famous Viṣṇu temple at Pandharpur in Maharaṣhtra. In fact, the word 'Viṭṭha' is a corrupted form of the word Viṣṇu. Rakumābāī (Rukmiṇī) is his consort standing by his left side.

This is the form of the Lord Viṣṇu revealed to a Brāhmaṇa, Puṇḍali by name because of his intense devotion to his parents.

Raṅganātha, along with Varadarāja of Kāñcīpuram and Veṅkaṭeśa of Tirupati, is the most popular aspect of Viṣṇu worshipped in South India. The well-known temple at Śrīraṅgam in Tamilnadu is the very heart of the Śrīvaiṣṇava cult. This temple—at least the original icon—

is said to have been born out of the ocean and given by Śrī Rāma to Vibhīṣaṇa. While carrying it from Ayodhyā to Laṅkā, Vibhīṣaṇa placed it on the ground at the present site, in order to rest a while. Unfortunately for him (and fortunately for others!) it got firmly fixed there!

The image is of the Yogaśayana type (lying on the serpent-bed in Yoga) with only two hands, the right hand apparently supporting the head while the left rests on the serpent-bed.

The lotus with Brahmā, the Āyudhapuruṣas (the weapons in human form), the demons Madhu and Kaiṭabha who were killed by him, as also some sages like Bhṛgu and Mārkandeya are often depicted along with the Lord.

Similar Yogaśayana images are found in Sriranga-patna of Karnataka and Tiruvanantapuram of Kerala where it is known as Padmanābha or Anantaśayana.

Varadarāja, the king among the bestowers of boons, is another aspect of Lord Viṣṇu which is very popular. Also known as Karivarada, it represents that aspect of the Lord responsible for saving Gajendra, the elephant king, from the death-clutches of the crocodile.

He is shown as riding on his vehicle Garuḍa and in the act of discharging the discus. The elephant Gajendra with its foot caught by the powerful teeth of the crocodile is also shown. Sometimes a human figure with its hands in obeisance is also shown near the crocodile, to represent the Gandharva (a demigod) who had been delivered from his curse which had resulted in his birth as a crocodile.

The temple of Śrī Varadarāja at Kāncīpuram in South India is one of the most important and famous Viṣṇu temples.

Veṅkaṭeśa, also known as Veṅkaṭeśvara Srīnivāsa or Bālāji of Tirupati in Andhra Pradesh is perhaps the most popular of all the Hindu deities in our country and the temple on the Tirupati hills gets fabulous income. The word Veṅgaḍam of Tamil origin signifies a hill. So Veṅkaṭeśa is the Lord of the hill. The story goes that Lord Visṇu as Varāha (the boar) decided to continue his stay on the earth and that Garuḍa brought down the hill of Vaikuṇṭha to earth for the Lord's residence. Lord Śrīnivāsa or Veṅkaṭeśa, another aspect of Viṣṇu, also manifested himself there at that time to reside on the earth for the good of mankind.

The image is said to be an Udbhavamūrti (spontaneously manifested) and does not conform to known Āgama traditions. As regards the exact nature and form of the image, doubts exist, some opining that it represents Harihara, and others considering it as Subrahmaṇya or even Devī.

Viṣvaksena or 'the all-conquering' is an aspect of Viṣṇu, which occupies the same place in Vaiṣṇava tradition as Gaṇeśa in the Śaiva tradition. He is worshipped at the beginning of any undertaking, to avoid obstacles. He is shown with four hands, wearing Śaṅkha, Cakra and Gadā in three hands and the fourth exhibiting the Tarjanīmudrā (threatening finger pose). The right leg is usually hanging down from the pedestal.

Viṣvaksena is also depicted sometimes as the gate-keeper or chief attendant of Lord Viṣṇu. He is shown standing on a white lotus and with long matted hair as also a beard. He represents the worldly sciences.

MINOR DEITIES ASSOCIATED WITH VIṢṆU

Garutmān or Garuḍa, the mighty bird-vehicle of Lord Viṣṇu is a minor deity invariably found in all the Vaiṣṇava temples. He is described as the son of the sage couple Kaśyapa and Vinatā and as the younger brother of Aruṇa, the charioteer of Sun-god. The chief among his multifarious exploits is his bringing of the pot of nectar from Indra's heaven. It is precisely this that made Lord Viṣṇu choose him as His vehicle.

Literally, the word Garuḍa means 'wings of speech'. He actually personifies Vedic knowledge. On his wings, as it were, Vedic Knowledge has come down to us, from the world of God.

The Garuḍa image is usually anthropomorphic. He is shown with a sharp beak, and two wings at the back. The hands may be eight or four or just two. Two of the hands are always in the adoration pose. In the others he carries the conch, wheel, mace, sword, snake and nectar-pot. The image is usually installed right opposite the central shrine.

It may appear to be rather intriguing that Lord Viṣṇu has a serpent as his couch and an eagle, its arch enemy, as his vehicle! This is to show that he is the Lord of balance and harmony which is an essential quality for one charged with the responsibility of sustaining this multifarious universe.

Another deity invariably found in the Viṣṇu temples, especially in the South, is Hanumān the monkey-god. The *Rāmāyaṇa* pictures him as a highly erudite, cultured and refined person. He is as strong as he is wise, and as devoted as he is strong and wise, a rare combination indeed.

He is represented in two postures: When in the company of Śrī Rāma, Sītā and Lakṣmaṇa, he is shown standing humbly at a distance or sitting devotedly at the feet of Śrī Rāma. In shrines specially erected for him, he strikes a heroic pose, usually with the mace in his left hand and carrying the Sañjīvinī mountain in his right hand.

Apart from these, it is common to show the weapons of Lord Viṣṇu also in human form. They are then called Āyudhapuruṣas (weapon-beings). The Āyudhapuruṣa may be male, female, or neuter, depending upon the gender of the word indicating it. For instance, Gadā (mace) is a female deity whereas the Cakra (discus) is a neuter deity.

The Sudarśana-cakra is shown as a person with a hexagon as his background, brilliant as fire and having four or eight or sixteen arms holding bow, arrow, trident, noose, goad and other implements as also weapons, apart from the usual Vaiṣṇavite symbols. It is said to represent the cosmic mind, the will of the Lord to multiply as well as His infinite power to create and destroy the universe. The Sudarśana-mantra is said to possess the power to neutralise poisons and exorcise malignant spirits.

The Kaumodakī, the Gadā (mace) of Lord Viṣṇu is depicted as a female deity, with one face and two hands which are in the posture of adoration. It symbolises power and sovereignty.

No account of Lord Viṣṇu will be complete without mentioning about the Śālagrāma, a blackish rounded and polished stone with a hole containing the fossils of tiny molluscs, which is worshipped as an emblem of His. There are several varieties of them representing different aspects of the Lord. Śālagrāmas can be installed in temples but are usually worshipped in one's own home privately. Once it is kept at home, its worship becomes obligatory.

7
THE TRINITY (Continued)

Śiva

Śiva is the last deity of the Trinity. He is responsible for the dissolution of the universe. He is the embodiment of Tamas, the centrifugal inertia, the tendency towards dispersion and annihilation.

Literally, Śiva is one in whom the Universe 'sleeps' after destruction and before the next cycle of creation.

All that is born, must die. All that is produced, must disintegrate and be destroyed. This is an inviolable law. The principle that brings about this disintegration, the power behind this destruction, is Śiva.

Śiva is much more than that. Disintegration of the universe ends in the ultimate thinning out, into a boundless void. This boundless void, the substratum of all existence, from which springs out again and again this apparently

Fig. 20. Śiva

limitless universe, is Śiva. So, though Śiva is described as responsible for destruction, he is equally responsible for creation and existence. In this sense, Brahmā and Viṣṇu are also Śiva. It is perhaps this identity that is revealed by some of the stories in the Purāṇas. If one story makes Śiva speak from the womb of the infinite pillar of fire to Brahmā and Viṣṇu that they are his own aspects, other stories make Śiva as being born from the brows of an angry Viṣṇu or from Brahmā who was intensely desiring to beget a son.

Though Śiva is often called Rudra, especially in his terrific aspect, whether the two are identical or not has been a subject of discussion and even controversy. Many scholars are inclined to think that the Rudra of the Vedas and the Śiva of the Purāṇas and Āgamas are two different deities fused into one at a later date as cultural integration of the two races accepting them progressed. According to these scholars Śiva the pacific deity is a non-Āryan god, 'more ancient' than the Vedic Rudra. Though the 'Āryan conquerors' despised and derided the Śaivas and their Śiva (apparently because of some of their mysterious rituals and practices) as the two races had to live together, rapproachment and consequent cultural reconciliation became inevitable.

Whatever may be the truth of these statements they are irrelevant to our study here, since we are more interested in discovering the significance of the symbology concerned, to enrich our lives.

Śiva is worshipped both in the anthropomorphic aspect and as the Liṅga, the latter being the rule whereas the former is an exception. The most common of his pictures and images shows him as a very handsome youth, white as camphor. His limbs besmeared with ashes are strong and smooth. He has three eyes—the third eye being on the forehead between the eyebrows—and four arms, two of the arms holding the Triśūla (trident) and Ḍamaru (drum) while the other two are in the Abhaya (protection-giving) and Varada (boon-giving) Mudrās (poses). He has a crown of long matted hair from which flows the river Gaṅgā. He also wears the crescent moon as a diadem. A tiger-skin and an elephant-skin adorn his body as his garments. There are serpents all over his body forming the necklace, the girdle, the Yajñopavīta (sacred thread) as also arm-bracelets. There is also a garland of skulls round his blue neck.

Man, being what he is, cannot help super-imposing his own states on his gods too! Therefore it is but natural for him to conceive of Śiva as a man with family. Pārvatī is his consort. Gaṇeśa and Kumāra (also known as Skanda or Subrahmaṇya) are his sons.

Then there is the large retinue forming a veritable zoo as it were! Nandi his vehicle bull, Bhṛṅgi the Ṛṣi with three legs and three arms, the mouse of Gaṇeśa, the peacock of Kumāra as also a host of ghosts, goblins and imps constantly capering round him—form his large retinue.

Though he has his headquarters in the icy mountains, the Himālayas, he is fond of roaming the earth, especially the burial grounds and cremation sites. All this is in perfect consonance with his nature as the Lord of destruction and dissolution.

Before embarking upon the explanation of all this, which is obviously symbolical, it is better to summarise first the various stories about Śiva recounted in our mythological literature.

(1) Once Pārvatī, in a playful mood, closed his two eyes, and lo! the entire world was plunged in darkness. To save the worlds from this predicament, Śiva willed a third eye in between his eyebrows, sending forth light, fire and heat. Later on, he opened this third eye—normally kept closed out of infinite mercy for humanity— to burn up Kāmadeva, the lord of lust.

(2) When the celestial river Gaṅgā, which was descending from the heaven to this earth, fell ferociously on Śiva's head out of pride, he just got her locked up there! Only after much prayer and supplication by Bhagīratha (who was responsible for bringing the celestial river down to this earth) and due apologies by Gaṅgā, did he allow her to stream out.

(3) When the Kṣīrasamudra, the ocean of milk, was being churned, one of the objects to rise was the cool crescent moon. Śiva seized it and made it his diadem. When the deadly poison Hālāhala also rose and started destroying the worlds with its leaping tongues of fire, Śiva gathered it on to his palm and drank it, thus saving the worlds. Pārvatī, getting alarmed about the safety of her spouse, pressed his throat so that the poison could not go down into the stomach! It thus remained in his throat, lending its blue colour permanently to it.

(4) Being angered by Śiva whose extraordinary beauty had attracted their wives, the Ṛṣis of Dārukavana

tried to kill him through sorcerous rituals. Out of the sacrificial fire rose a tiger, a deer and a red-hot iron. Siva killed the tiger and wore its skin, caught hold of the deer with his left hand (which has remained there ever since) and made the iron one of this weapons.

(5) Other stories relate to his destroying the sacrifice of Dakṣa, his cutting off, of one of the five heads of Brahmā for having spoken disrespectfully, his destroying the three cities built by the demon Tripurāsura, his killing the elephant demon Gajāsura and wearing his hide, his having granted to Arjuna as a boon the weapon Pāśupatāstra, his having become Ardhanārīśvara to dispel the ignorance of his devotee Bhṛṅgi, his apearing as a pillar of fire to teach a lesson to Brahmā and Viṣṇu, his vanquishing Yama, the god of death, to save his votary Mārkaṇḍeya, and so on.

An attempt can now be made to unravel this mysterious symbology of the Śiva-picture. Śiva is snow-white in colour, which matches wonderfully with that of his abode, the Himālayas. White stands for light that dispels darkness, knowledge that dispels ignorance. He is the very personification of cosmic consciousness. It may appear strange that Śiva who represents Tamas (the force of darkness and destruction) is pictured as white, whereas Viṣṇu who represents Sattva (the force of light and enlightenment) is pictured as dark! There is nothing strange in this since the opposing Guṇas are inseparable. Hence Śiva is white outside and dark inside whereas Viṣṇu is the reverse of it.

The three eyes of Śiva represent the sun, the moon and the fire, the three sources of light, life and heat. The third eye can also indicate the eye of knowledge and wisdom and hence his omniscience.

If the sun and the moon form his two eyes as it were, then the whole sky including the powerful wind blowing in it, forms his hair. That is why he is called Vyomakeśa (one who has the sky or space as his hair).

Tiger is a ferocious animal that mercilessly devours its hapless victims. Desire, which consumes human beings, without ever being satiated, can be compared to a tiger. That Śiva has killed the tiger and wears its skin as his apparel shows his complete mastery over desire.

The elephant being a powerful animal, wearing its skin implies that Śiva has completely subjugated all animal impulses.

The garland of skulls (Muṇḍamālā) that he wears and the ashes of the funeral pyre with which he has besmeared his body indicate that he is the lord of destruction. The garland of skulls also represents the revolution of ages and successive appearance and disappearance of the human races.

Śiva is the lord of Yoga and Yogis. He is often shown as sitting in deep meditation immersed in the enjoyment of the bliss of his own self. The water of the river Gaṅgā represents this. Or it can represent Jñāna, knowledge. Since Gaṅgā is highly adored as a great purifying agent, it goes without saying that he whom it adorns, is the very personification of purifying or redeeming power.

The crescent moon stands for time, since measurement of time as days or months depends upon the waxing and waning of the moon. By wearing it as a diadem, Śiva is showing us that even the all-powerful time is only an ornament for him!

And then, the snakes. The venomous cobras which symbolise death for us adorn his frame in all possible manner embellishing it further. He alone, to whom symbol of death is a decoration, can gulp down the deadly poison Hālāhala to save the worlds. All this points to one thing: he is Mṛtyuñjaya, the conqueror of death! Coiled serpents may also represent cycles of time in the macrocosm and the basic energy—akin to sexual energy—of living beings in the microcosm. So, Śiva is the master of time and energy.

Iconographically Śiva may have two, three, four, eight, ten or even thirty-two hands. Some of the various objects shown in these hands are: Triśūla (trident), Cakra (discus), Paraśu (battleaxe), Ḍamaru (drum), Akṣamālā (rosary), Mṛga (deer), pāśa (noose), Daṇḍa (staff), Pināka or Ajagava (bow), Khatvāṅga (magic wand) Pāśupata (spear), Padma (lotus), Kapāla (skull-cup), Darpaṇa, (mirror), Khaḍga (sword) and so on. It is rather difficult to find a meaning for everyone of these items. However an attempt will be made to explain some of them.

The Triśūla (trident) being an important weapon of offence and defence, indicates that Śiva is the supreme ruler. Philosophically it can stand for the three Guṇas or the three processes of creation, preservation and dissolution. Hence Śiva the wielder of the trident is the master of the Guṇas and from him proceed the cosmic processes.

It is said that while dancing the Tāṇḍavanṛtya Śiva sounded his Ḍamaru (small drum) fourteen times, thereby producing sounds like a-i-uṇ, r-lṛ-k and so on, which are now known as the *Māheśvarasūtras,* the fourteen basic formulae containing all the alphabets arranged in the most ingenious manner, facilitating innumerable grammatical processes. Hence the Ḍamaru represents the alphabets, grammar (the science of language) or language itself. In other words it stands for all words—spoken or written or otherwise expressed—and hence for the entire gamut of all arts and sciences, sacred and secular. It also represents sound as such, the logos, from which entire creation has proceeded. By holding it in his hand, Śiva is demonstrating the fact that the entire creation, including its various arts and sciences, has proceeded out of his will, his play.

If the Akṣamālā (rosary) shows that he is the master of spiritual sciences, the Khaṭvāṅga (magic wand with a skull fixed at one end) shows that he is an adept in occult sciences too. The Kapāla (skull-cup) with which he drinks blood, is another symbol that points to his all-destroying power. The Darpaṇa (mirror) indicates that the entire creation is just a reflection of his cosmic form.

The icon of Śiva is never worshipped as the Mūlamūrti (original, installed in the sānctum sānctorum), but only as an Utsavamūrti (the icon used during festivals for taking out in a procession).

SIVALIṄGA

As regards the Liṅga, the emblem of Śiva universally venerated, some explanation is needed. Literally Śiva means auspiciousness and Liṅga means a sign or symbol. Hence the 'Śivaliṅga' is just a symbol of the great God of the universe ('Mahādeva') who is all-auspiciousness. As already explained (p. 57), 'Śiva' means the one in whom the whole creation sleeps after dissolution. 'Liṅga' also means the same thing—a place where created objects get dissolved during the disintegration of the created universe. Since, according to Hinduism, it is the same God that creates, sustains and destroys the universe, the Śivaliṅga represents symbolically God Himself.

Whether the Śivaliṅga is a phallic emblem or not, is a moot point. Phallic cults have existed in all countries and in all civilizations. It is quite likely that the phallic cults of an aboringinal civilization were absorbed into Hinduism and the worship itself was elevated to honour the Father-Mother-Principle of creation. This is one view. That it is a remnant of the Vedic Yūpastambha, to which sacrificial victims used to be tied, is another view. According to this view, the Hindu temple is a metamorphosis of the Vedic Yāgaśālā (sacrificial shed). That it is an imitation of the Buddhist stūpa is another guess that is sometimes hazarded but not subtantiated, since Śivaliṅgas have been found even in the pre-Buddhistic civilizations of Harappa and Mohenjo Daro.

Since God is beyond name and form, and since we cannot conceive of an abstract principle like Him, without the aid of concrete symbols, a rounded surface is perhaps the nearest approach to him.

Śivaliṅgas may be Cala (movable) or Acala (immovable). The Cala-Liṅgas may be kept in the shrine of one's own home for worship or prepared temporarily with materials like clay or dough etc., for worship and dispensed with after the worship or worn on the body as Iṣṭaliṅga as the Vīraśaivas do. The Acala-liṅgas are those installed in temples. They are usually made of stone and have three parts. The lowest part which is square, is called Brahma-bhāga and represents Brahmā, the creator. The middle part which is octagonal, is called Viṣṇu-bhāga and represents Viṣṇu, the sustainer. These two parts are embedded inside the pedestal. The Rudrabhāga which is cylindrical and projects outside the pedestal is the one to which worship is offered. Hence it is called Pūjābhāga.

The Pūjābhāga also contains certain lines technically called Brahmasūtra, without which the Liṅga becomes unfit for worship.

ASPECTS OF LORD ŚIVA

Comparable to the Vyūhas or emanations of Lord Viṣṇu, is the Pañcānana form of Lord Śiva. Pañcānana or the five-faced one represents the five aspects of Śiva vis-a-vis the created universe. The five faces are respectively Īśāna, Tatpuruṣa, Aghora, Vāmadeva and Sadyojāta. The face Īśāna turned towards the zenith, represents the highest aspect and is also called Sadāśiva. On the physical plane, it represents the power that rules over ether or sky and on the spiritual plane, it is the deity that grants Mokṣa or liberation. Tatpuruṣa facing east, stands for the power that rules over air and represents the forces of darkness and obscuration on the spiritual plane. Aghora, facing south and ruling over the element fire, stands for the power that absorbs and renovates the universe. Vāmadeva facing north, ruling over the element water, is responsible for preservation. Sadyojāta, facing west represents the power that creates.

Iconographically, all the five aspects are shown in different ways.

There are several other aspects in which Lord Śiva is depicted or worshipped. These can be broadly divided into the following categories: (1) Saumya or Anugraha Mūrti; (2) Ugra, Raudra or Samhāra Mūrtis; (3) Nṛtta or Tāṇḍava Mūrti; (4) Dakṣiṇāmūrti; (5) Liṇgodbhavamūrti; (6) Bhikṣāṭanamūrti; (7) Haryardhamūrti; (8) Ardhanārīsvaramūrti.

Peaceful form of Śiva as also the form showing mercy and grace belong to the first group. The forms showing grace or granting boons to Caṇḍeśa, Nandīśvara, Vighneśvara or Rāvaṇa belong to this category.

All terrific aspects can be classed under the second group. Kaṅkāla Bhairava represents Śiva who cut off the fifth head of Brahmā for having reviled him and who had to wander as a beggar for twelve years to get rid of that sin. Gajāsuravadhamūrti represents him as killing the demon Nīla (an associate of Andhakāsura) who had assumed the form of an elephant. Tripurāntaka-mūrti depicts him as destroying by his arrow, the three cities of iron, silver and gold built on the earth, in air and in heaven by the three sons of Andhakāsura who had become almost invincible because of these three impregnable shelters. Śarabheśamūrti pictures Śiva as a Śarabha (an imaginary animal more ferocious than the lion) destroying the Narasiṁha form of Viṣṇu, a story obviously conceived by the Śaivites to assert the superiority of their Lord over Viṣṇu!

Kālāri-mūrti portrays him as vanquishing Yama, the god of death, who wanted to take away the life of Mārkaṇḍeya, a great devotee of Śiva. Kāmāntakamūrti illustrates him as destroying Kāma, the god of lust, by the fire emitted through his third eye. Andhakāsura-vadha-mūrti shows him as vanquishing Andhakāsura and later on, on supplication, conferring on him the commandership of the Gaṇas (dwarf attendants). Andhaka became Bhṛṅgīśa.

Lord Śiva is a great master of dance. All the 108 modes of dancing known to the treatises on dancing have come from him. It is said that he dances every evening in order to relieve the sufferings of creatures and entertain the gods who gather in Kailāsa in full strength. (Hence he is called Sabhāpati, the lord of the congregation.)

Only nine modes of dancing are described of which the Naṭarāja aspect is the most well-known. The Naṭarāja icon shows him with four hands and two legs, in the posture of dancing. There is the Ḍamaru (drum) in the upper right hand and fire in the left. The lower right hand is in Abhayamudrā (pose of protection) and the left is pointing towards the uplifted left foot. The left foot is resting on the demon Apasmārapuruṣa. The whole image may or may not be surrounded by a circle of blazing fire.

Śiva's dance indicates a continuous process of creation, preservation and destruction. The Ḍamaru represents the principle of Śabda (sound) and hence Ākāśa (ether), which proceeds immediately from the Ātman and is responsible for further creation or evolution. Fire represents Pralayāgni, the fire that destroys the world at the time of dissolution of the world, and hence symbolises the

Fig. 21. Naṭarāja

process of destruction. Thus Ḍamaru and fire represent the continuous cycle of creation, preservation and destruction. The other two hands indicate that he who takes refuge at the feet of the Lord will have nothing to fear. The Apasmāra-puruṣa (Apasmāra=epilepsy) symbolises ignorance which makes us lose our balance and consciousness. He is trampled upon by the Lord for the good of the devotees who take refuge.

Several other dancing postures of Śiva like Ānanda-tāṇḍava-mūrti, Umā-taṇḍava-mūrti, Tripura-tāṇḍava-mūrti, and Ūrdhva-tāṇḍava-mūrti are also mentioned in the Āgamas.

Śiva is as great a master of Yoga and spiritual sciences as he is of music, dancing and other arts. As a universal teacher he is called Dakṣiṇāmūrti. Since Śiva was seated facing south (dakṣiṇa=south) when he taught the sages in a secluded spot on the Himālayas, he is called Dakṣiṇāmūrti. He has three eyes and four arms and one of the legs is trampling upon the Āpasmārapuruṣa. Two of the arms (the front right and the front left) are in Jñānamudra and Varadamudra poses (showing the imparting of knowledge and bestowing of gifts). The back hands hold the Akṣamālā (rosary) and, either fire or ṣerpent. He is the very model of the perfect Guru. He is surrounded by several Ṛṣis eager to learn Ātmavidyā (Self-knowledge) from him.

Śiva is said to have appeared as a blazing pillar of fire, of immeasurable size, to destroy the pride of Brahmā and Viṣṇu. Liṅgodhbavamūrti depicts him as manifesting in the heart of the Liṅga. The image has four arms. Brahmā and Viṣṇu stand on either side adoring him.

Fig. 22. Dakṣiṇāmūrti

Fig. 23. Haryardhamūrti

Fig. 24. Ardhanārīśvara

The Bhikṣāṭanamūrti shows Śiva as a naked Bhairava, begging his food in the skull cup. It is almost the same as the Kaṅkālamūrti.

The Haryardha-mūrti, also called as Hari-hara and Śaṅkaranārāyaṇa, has Śiva on the right half and Viṣṇu on the left. A fusion of these two aspects into one god is an obvious attempt at a happy reconciliation of the warring cults of Śiva and Viṣṇu.

The Ardhanāriśvara (half man and half woman) form with Pārvatī as the left half represents the bipolar nature of the created world and hence the need to look upon woman as equal and complementary to man.

MINOR DEITIES ASSOCIATED WITH ŚIVA

There can be no Śiva temple without Nandi, the recumbent bull placed in front of the shrine. Nandi or Nandikeśvara may be depicted exactly like Śiva—with three eyes and two hands holding the Paraśu (battle axe) and Mṛga (the antelope). But the other two hands are joined together in the Añjali pose (obeisance). More commonly he is shown as a bull-faced human being or just as a bull.

The Purāṇas describe him as born out of the right side of Viṣṇu resembling Śiva exactly and given as a son to the sage Sālaṅkāyana who had practised severe austerities. Other versions describe him as the son of the sage Śilāda who got him by the grace of Śiva.

Nandikeśvara, also known as Adhikāranandi, is the head of the Gaṇas of Śiva and also his Vāhana (carrier vehicle).

Symbolically, the bull represents the animal intincts, especially the sex, and Śiva's riding on it reflects his absolute mastery over it.

Then comes Bhṛṅgi, the sage, who was singularly devoted to Lord Śiva, and was elevated to the retinue of Śiva's abode. The sage was so fanatical in his devotion to Śiva that he did not care even for Pārvatī, his consort! When Pārvatī merged herself into the body of Śiva and Śiva thus became Ardhanārīśvara, Bhṛṅgi was still so bigoted that he became a Bhṛṅga (=bee) and bored through the centre of the Ardhanārīśvara form to complete his circumambulation! Hence the name Bhṛṅgi. Siva, of course, made him realise his mistake.

Vīrabhadra is another deity associated with Śiva. He is the personification of Śiva's anger manifested during Dakṣa's sacrifice because of the contemptuous treatment meted out to him. Śiva is said to have created him out of a hair plucked out from his head. Vīrabhadra successfully destroyed Dakṣa's sacrifice and humiliated all the gods who had assembled there. He is usually shown with three eyes and four arms holding bow, arrow, sword and mace. He wears a garland of skulls. The face is terrific. Bhadrakālī, his counterpart created by Pārvatī, is sometimes shown by his side. Śiva temples may have a small shrine dedicated to him, located usually in the south-east.

Next comes Caṇḍeśvara, a human devotee raised to the status of a deity, by Lord Śiva because of his intense devotion. He is a fierce deity holding weapons of war and destruction like the bow, arrow, trident, chisel, noose and so on. Though independent shrines dedicated to him are not uncommon, he is usually installed in every Śiva temple in the north-eastern corner, facing south. Devotees believe that he can act as a messenger and mediator interceding with the Lord on behalf of the devotees. Hence supplication before him is a duty of every devotee visiting the Śiva temples.

Other attendants of Śiva are the Gaṇas, also known as Pramathagaṇas or Bhūtagaṇas (demigods or malignant spirits). If they are not propitiated, they can do harm.

8

ŚAKTI OR THE DIVINE POWER AS THE GODDESS

The universe that we see and experience is a bundle of energy, both packed and unpacked. This is the discovery of modern science, which incidentally, has demolished the distinction between matter and energy. According to it, there is one basic energy behind all forms of matter and energy. However, it seems to be still far off from discovering the relationship between matter on the one hand, and, mind and life on the other. Are they also, though apparently poles apart, manifestations of the same basic energy? Could it be that the same energy or matter, at one level of vibration is called 'matter', at another, 'mind' and yet another, 'life'? Modern science or the modern scientists, devoting most of their attention to the manifest material universe may not even be prepared to concede this possibility! Hindu philosophy, based on the Vedānta and a group of works based on the Vedānta and more commonly known as the Tantras* postulates exactly this! The source and sustenance of all creation, whether at the level of matter or

* Tantras are a vast body of Hindu religious literature devoted to expounding the cult of the Divine Mother.

life or mind, is one and one only. It is Śakti (=energy). Brahman (the Absolute) of the Vedānta and Śakti or Devī of the Tantras are identical. When that 'energy' is in a static condition, with neither evolution nor involution, when the universe to be created is not even in a seed-form as it were, it is called Brahman. When it starts evolving into this creation, sustains it and withdraws it back into itself, it is called Śakti. If Brahman is the coiled serpent in sleep, Śakti is the same serpent in motion. If Brahman is likened to the word, Śakti is its meaning. If Brahman is like fire, Śakti is its burning power. The two are inseparable: one in two and two in one.

In the Hindu mythological literature, as also in the Tantras, this energy is always pictured as a female deity, the Devī, as the consort of its counterpart male deity. Each member of the Trinity has his Śakti or Devī as his consort: Sarasvatī of Brahmā, Lakṣmī of Viṣṇu and Pārvatī of Śiva. However, the mother-cult that has evolved over the last few centuries, is predominantly centred round Pārvatī, the consort of Śiva.

Mother-worship and mother-cult are not alien to the Vedic religion as some suggest. The concept of Aditi, the mother of gods, personification of nature and the *Ambhṛṇīsūkta* as also the *Rātrīsūkta* of the *Ṛgveda* clearly contain the origins of mother-worship.

Sarasvatī

Sarasvatī is the Śakti, the power and the consort of Brahmā the creator. Hence she is the procreatrix, the mother, of the entire creation.

Fig. 25. Sarasvatī

Literally Sarasvatī means 'the flowing one'. In the *Ṛgveda* she represents a river and the deity presiding over it. Hence, she is connected with fertility and purification. Here are some of the names used to describe her: Sāradā (giver of essence), Vāgīśvarī (mistress of speech), Brāhmī (wife of Brahmā), Mahāvidyā (knowledge supreme) and so on. It is obvious that the concept of Sarasvatī, developed by the later mythological literature is already here. The 'flowing one' can represent speech also if taken in an allegorical sense. Hence Sarasvatī represents power and intelligence from which organized creation proceeds.

She is considered as the personification of all knowledge—arts, sciences, crafts, and skills. Knowledge is the antithesis of the darkness of ignorance. Hence she is depicted as pure white in colour. Since she is the representation of all sciences, arts, crafts and skills she has to be extraordinarily beautiful and graceful. Clad in a spotless white apparel and seated on a lotus seat, she holds in her four hands a Vīṇā (lute), Akṣamālā (rosary) and Pustaka (book). Though these are most common, there are several variations. Some of the other objects shown are: Pāśa (noose), Aṅkuśa (goad), Padma (lotus), Triśūla (trident), Śaṅkha (conch), Cakra (discus) and so on. Occasionally she is shown with five faces or with eight hands. Even three eyes or blue neck are not uncommon. In this case she is the Mahāsarasvatī aspect of Durgā or Pārvatī.

Though no separate carrier vehicle is mentioned, Haṁsa or swan, the vehicle of Brahmā, her spouse, is usually associated with her also. In popular mythological literature and pictures, a peacock is also shown as her carrier vehicle.

Coming to the symbology: Being the consort of Brahmā the creator, she represents his power and intelligence, without which organized creation is impossible. To show that this intelligent power is stupendous and absolutely pure, she is pictured as white and dazzling.

As usual, the four arms show her unimpeded power in all directions or her all-pervasiveness.

Being the goddess of learning, it is but proper that Sarasvatī is shown holding a book in her left hand. The book represents all areas of secular sciences. Mere intellectual learning, without a heart tempered by higher feelings, sentiments and emotions, is as dry as saw-dust. So she holds a Vīṇā (lute) on which she actually plays, to show the need for the cultivation of fine-arts. Then there is the Akṣamāla (rosary) held in the right hand. This symbolises all spiritual sciences or Yoga including Tapas (austerities), meditation and Japa (repetition of the divine name). By holding the book in the left hand and the rosary in the right hand she is obviously teaching us that spiritual sciences are more important than secular sciences.

The peacock with its beautiful plumage stands for this world in all its glory. Since the attractions of the world lead the spiritual aspirant astray, the peacock can actually symbolise Avidyā (ignorance or nescience). On the other hand the swan, which is supposed to possess the peculiar power of separating milk from water, stands for Viveka (wisdom, discrimination) and hence for Vidyā (knowledge). Though it is true that Vidyā or Parāvidyā (spiritual illumination) alone can give us Mokṣa (beatitude), Avidyā signifying secular knowledge—the sciences and arts of the world—need not be and should not be neglected. As the Īśāvāsya Upaniṣad (11) puts it,* we transcend hunger and thirst through the secular sciences and then alone can obtain immortality through the spiritual sciences. It is to teach this great truth to us that Mother Sarasvatī has chosen the two carrier vehicles, the swan and the peacock.

Lakṣmī

For obvious reasons, Lakṣmī, the goddess of fortune, is more sought after than Sarasvatī, the goddess of learning. Being the power and consort of Viṣṇu, the preserver, she is represented as the power of multiplicity and the goddess of fortune, both of which are equally necessary in the process of preservation.

'Śrī' or 'Lakṣmī', as depicted in the Vedas, is the goddess of wealth and fortune, power and beauty. Though there is scope for the supposition that Śrī and Lakṣmī are two separate deities, the descriptions of them are so identical, that we are tempted to conclude that they represent one and the same deity. Some scholars opine that 'Śrī' was a pre-Vedic deity connected with fertility, water and agriculture. She was later fused with Lakṣmī, the Vedic goddess of beauty.

In her first incarnation, according to the Purāṇas, she was the daughter of the sage Bhṛgu and his wife Khyāti. She was later born out of the ocean of milk at the time of

---

* 'Avidyayā mṛtyuṁ tīrtvā vidyayāmṛtamaśnute'.

Fig. 26. Lakṣmī

its churning. She, being the consort of Viṣṇu, is born as his spouse whenever he incarnates. When he appeared as Vāmana, Paraśurāma, Rāma and Kṛṣṇa, she appeared as Padmā (or Kamalā), Dharaṇī, Sītā and Rukmiṇī. She is as inseparable from Viṣṇu as speech from meaning or knowledge from intellect, or good deeds from righteousness. He represents all that is masculine, and she, all that is feminine.

Lakṣmī is usually described as enchantingly beautiful and standing on a lotus, and holding lotuses in each of her two hands. It is because of this, perhaps, that she is named as Padmā or Kamalā. She is also adorned with a lotus garland. Very often elephants are shown on either side, emptying pitchers of water over her, the pitchers being presented by celestial maidens. Her colour is variously described as dark, pink, golden yellow or white. While in the company of Viṣṇu, she is shown with two hands only. When worshipped in a temple—separate temples for Lakṣmī are rather rare—she is shown seated on a lotus throne, with four hands holding Padma, Śaṅkha, Amṛtakalaśa (pot of ambrosia) and Bilva fruit. Sometimes, another kind of fruit, the Mahāliṅga (a citron) is shown instead of Bilva. When shown with eight hands, bow and arrow, mace and discus are added. This is actually the Mahālakṣmī, an aspect of Durgā.

We can now attempt an explanation that is behind this highly symbolical picture. If Lakṣmī is pictured as dark in complexion, it is to show that she is the consort of Viṣṇu, the dark god. If golden yellow, that shows her as the source of all wealth. If white, she represents the purest form of

Prakṛti (nature) from which the universe had developed. The pinkish complexion, which is more common, reflects her compassion for creatures, since she is the mother of all.

Her four hands signify her power to grant the four Puruṣārthas (ends of human life), Dharma (righteousness), Artha (wealth), Kāma (pleasures of the flesh), and Mokṣa (beatitude).

The lotuses, in various stages of blooming, represent the worlds and beings in various stages of evolution.

The fruit stands for the fruits of our labours. How-ever– much we may toil and labour, unless the Mother is gracious enough to grant the fruits of our labour, nothing will be of any avail. If the fruit is a coconut—with its shell, kernel and water—it means that from her originate the three levels of creation, the gross, the subtle and the extremely subtle. If it is a pomegranate or a citron, it signifies that the various created worlds are under her control and that she transcends them all. If it is a bilva fruit—which, incidentally, is not very tasty or attractive, but which is extremely good for health—it stands for Mokṣa, the highest fruit of spiritual life.

Amṛtakalaśa also signifies the same thing, viz., that she can give us the bliss of immortality.

In some of the sculptural depictions of Lakṣmī, the owl is shown as her carrier-vehicle. It looks rather odd and strange that the goddess of fortune and beauty should have an ugly bird, the very sight of which is considered inauspicious, as her carrier! Once the symbolical significance of this oddity is unravelled, we will be in a better position to appreciate the poor bird and its compassionate mistress!

The word is Sanskrit for the owl is Ulūka. Ulūka is also one of the names of Indra, the king of gods! Hence Lakṣmī being the goddess of fortune could not have found a better person to ride on, than the king of gods, who personifies all the wealth, power and glory that a living being can aspire for in life. At the same time, here is a warning administered to the seekers of secular wealth, instead of spiritual wealth, by comparing even the glory of Indra to the ugliness of an inelegant and partially blind bird.

Based on the beautiful description given in the *Bhagavadgitā* (2.69) we can be generous enough to compare our owl to the Sthitaprajña, the man of steady wisdom. Then, the symbol would mean that Mother Lakṣmī is the mistress of spiritual wisdom. If we are not so generous, then, we can learn a lesson from it in another way, viz., 'Do not shut out your eyes to the light of wisdom coming from the sun of knowledge!' Out of consideration for mankind, the all-compassionate Mother has kept this personification of ignorance under her control.

SAMUDRAMATHANA
(Churning of the Ocean)

It may be interesting and even instructive to digress a little and deal with the story of Samudramathana (churning of the ocean of milk). Indra, the king of gods, lost his all to the demons, due to the disrespect shown out of pride, to a great sage Durvāsas. Lord Viṣṇu advised him to make up with his enemies (the demons) and with their help, to churn the ocean of milk, out of which Amṛta (ambrosia) could be got. By drinking it, the gods could become immortal and regain their lost sovereignty. Accordingly, the gods and the demons started churning the ocean, making the Mandara mountain as the churning rod and Vāsuki, the great serpent as the rope. Viṣṇu took the form of a gigantic tortoise (Kūrma) to support the mount Mandara from sinking. The first product of this joint venture and adventure was Hālāhala, the most deadly poison! Śiva the auspicious one, swallowed this, thus saving the worlds from sure destruction. Then were produced Kāmadhenu (the wish-yielding cow), Uccaiśravas (the white horse), Airāvata (the elephant), Kaustubhamaṇi (the matchless jewel), Kalpavṛkṣa (the wish-fulfilling tree), Lakṣmī (the goddess of fortune), Surā or Vāruṇī (the goddess of wine) and Dhanvantari (the physician of the gods) bearing the vessel of Amṛta (the ambrosia) in his hands. The Ṛṣis took away the cow Kāmadhenu, Bali (the king of demons) cast his eye on the horse Uccaiśravas, Indra (the king of gods) accepted the elephant Airāvata and got the tree Kalpavṛkṣa planted in his garden in heaven. Viṣṇu chose to wear the jewel Kaustubha on his chest whereas Lakṣmī chose Viṣṇu's chest as her dwelling. The gods chose Surā who had been, strangely enough, rejected by the demons. Contravening the original agreement that the Amṛta should be shared by both the groups equally, the demons forcibly snatched away the pot from Dhanvantari's hands to appropriate the entire quantity for themselves. Selfishness and greed, however, led to disagreement, discontent and conflcit. Taking this opportunity Viṣṇu took the form of Mohinī, the enchantress, lured the vessel of ambrosia into his hands and cleverly managed to distribute its contents among the gods only. Then the inevitable happened. Being intoxicated by the new strength gained thus, the gods fell upon the demons, vanquished them and regained their lost sovereignty.

This myth has great lessons for us. In order to get the greatest good of the greatest number, the saner elements of the society should influence the masses to bury their hatchet, sink all their petty differences and make a coordinated and co-operative effort to achieve it. Since the task is stupendous, the effort will have to be equally stupendous. The early results of all such joint ventures need not always be good or pleasant. Due to conflict of personalities and clash of interests which naturally arise in the field of joint ventures, it is Hālāhala that appears first and not Amṛta! This deadly poison starts destroying all the parties involved in the conflicts irrespective of who is right or who is wrong! Hence out of sheer necessity, the entire society should unite and appeal to the leaders to save it. Any true leader of the society, worth the name, will, like Śiva the auspicious one, voluntarily and willingly come forward risking his life to assimilate this poison and save the society from sure destruction. Once these conflicts are resolved and the efforts are redoubled, Lakṣmī signifying Abhyudaya (well-being, fortune) and Amṛta signifying Niśśreyasa (moral and spiritual elevation ultimately leading to beatitude) are bound to arise from the firmament of their joint adventure. But, again, contrary to the convenant, if the selfish and belligerent groups of the society try to appropriate to themselves all the fruits of the common labours,

God, the law-giver and justice personified, will thwart their efforts. The good shall and will vanquish the evil.

This story can be interpreted at the subjective level also. Anyone who is tired of the vicissitudes of life and is hankering for peace and bliss should seek it only in the highest spiritual enlightenment. Amṛta signifies just this enlightenment. To get this, an all-out effort will have to be made. The sense-organs which usually pull the mind down and create confusion, conflicts and heart-burns, should be tactfully mobilised in this effort even as the demons were used by the gods. Spiritual life is a long struggle. Meditation is actually mind-churning. Hence, this process will inevitably throw up the deadly poison hidden in the recesses of the mind as passions and prejudices, which try to destroy the every process of Sādhanā (spiritual efforts). An intense and earnest prayer to God, Śiva, will save the situation by getting it sublimated. The conquest of Māra by the Buddha or Satan by Christ, can be understood in this light. Once the worst is over, the spiritual aspirant will gradually start reaping the benefits of his efforts in the form of Siddhis (powers), psychic or otherwise. Kāmadhenus and Kalpavṛkṣas can mean such powers. This will be crowned with success when he gets a vision of the all-pervading cosmic energy (Lakṣmī) resulting in immortal bliss (Amṛta).

ASPECTS OF LAKṢMĪ

Eight forms of Lakṣmī, known as Aṣṭamahālakṣmī, are recognized in iconographical works. Out of these, Gajalakṣmī is the most popular. She is usually figured on the lintels of door frames. She is seated on an eight-petalled lotus, has four hands and is carrying a lotus, a pot of nectar, a bilva fruit and a conch. Behind her two elephants are shown pouring water over her from pots held in their trunks.

When the same goddess has two hands, she is called Sāmānyalakṣmī, or Indralakṣmī.

If she is depicted with two lotuses in two hands, and the other two hands display the Abhaya and Varada mudrās, she is designated as Varalakṣmī.

The other forms are not so common.

EIGHT ŚAKTIS OF VIṢṆU

The protecting power of Viṣṇu has eight aspects and each of these is pictured as a goddess.

Śrīdevī is the goddess of wealth and fortune. Bhūdevī, representing the earth, and often with Śrīdevī, as the junior consort of Viṣṇu, stands for sovereignty over the earth. Sarasvatī signifies learning. Prīti is love personified. Kīrti and Śānti give fame and peace whereas Tuṣṭi and Puṣṭi grant pleasure and strength.

ALAKṢMĪ

Alakṣmī is the opposite number of Lakṣmī. She is misfortune personified. She was also born during the churning of the ocean. Since she appeared earlier than Lakṣmī and hence elder, she is also called Jyeṣṭhā (the elder one). A sage, Dussaha (=the unbearable) by name, married her. According to another version, it was the sage Kapila. Adharma (unrighteousness) is her son. She is pictured as an old hag riding an ass. She has a broom in her hand. A crow adorns her banner. Her image finds a place in some temples. When propitiated, she can dispel evil and grant prosperity!

Sometimes Jyeṣṭhādevī is identified with Lakṣmī herself.

Since the created world is a mixture of opposites and things happen in cyclic order both fortune and misfortune are the two sides of the same coin. Being part and parcel of this creation and hence of our life, misfortune is no less divinely ordained than fortune. It is perhaps to teach us this great fact of life that even misfortune has been deified.

Pārvatī

Pārvatī is the power and consort of Śiva, the god of disintegration and destruction. An overwhelming majority of the goddesses of Hinduism are aspects and variations of Pārvatī. The names by which she is known or worshipped are too numerous to mention. If some of the names like Pārvatī, Haimavatī, Girijā and Dākṣāyaṇī indicate her origin from the Himālayas or Dakṣa (one of the forefathers of mankind), other names like Śivā, Mṛḍānī, Rudrāṇī and Śarvāṇī stress her aspect as the spouse of Śiva. Still other like Aparṇā and Umā have specific references to certain stories in the Paurāṇic literature.

One of the earliest references to this deity is found in the *Kenopaniṣad* (3.12) where she is mentioned as 'Umā Haimavatī' enlightening Indra, the king of gods, about Brahman, the Absolute or God. This reference is enough to conclude that the worship of this goddess is very ancient.

Fig. 27. Pārvatī

According to the Paurāṇic accounts, in her 'first' incarnation, she was Dākṣāyaṇī, the daughter of Dakṣa and Prasūti, and married to Lord Śiva. Unable to understand Lord Śiva's greatness, Dakṣa once reviled him and started harbouring hatred towards him. When he undertook the performance of a great sacrifice, the notable exception among the dignitaries invited was Śiva himself. Much against the advice of her spouse Dākṣayaṇī went to the sacrifice uninvited and being slighted, ended her life by igniting herself through the fire of yoga. Hence she came to be known as Satī, the chaste one. She was next reborn as Pārvatī, the daughter of Himavāṇ and Menā. After performing intense austerities she succeeded in pleasing Śiva and making him accept her again as his consort.

During the performance of these severe austerities, she refused to eat even dry leaves to sustain herself and hence got the appellation Aparṇā. Her mother Menā unable to see her dear daughter languishing by austerities, tried to dissuade her by the words, 'U mā' (=my dear, don't do like this!) which became her another name (Umā). Being the daughter of the Himālayas (the abode of snow) she has to be Gaurī (the white one). As the mother of the universe she is Ambā and Ambikā, both the words meaning 'mother'.

Like her consort Śiva, she also has two aspects: the mild and the terrible. As Pārvatī or Umā she represents the mild aspect. In this aspect she is usually shown with Śiva. Then she has only two hands, the right one holding a blue lotus and the left hanging loosely by the side. The image is richly decorated. When represented independently she is shown with four hands, two hands holding red and blue lotuses and the other two exhibiting the Varada and Abhaya Mudrās.

Though all the female deities are called Śaktis of their male counterparts, the words 'Śakti' and 'Devī' are more particularly—or even exclusively—used to denote the Śakti of Śiva, the innumerable aspects of Pārvatī. Considering Śiva as Mahādeva, the Supreme God, Pārvatī represents his power by which the universe is created, sustained and destroyed.

The Himālayas represent the Ākāśa or ether, the first fundamental substance. Menā stands for intelligence. Hence Pārvatī their offspring, represents the conscious substance of the universe. That is why she is also called Umā (=light, the bright one).

At the subjective level, Umā-Haimavatī represents Brahmavidyā or spiritual wisdom, by which union with Śiva or God, is attained.

Being the consort of Śiva, who is Rudra, the terrible, she also has her terrible aspects which need a separate study.

It is interesting to note that the Vaiṣṇava symbols—Śaṅkha and Cakra—are often shown in her hands also. Though the Purāṇas describe her as the sister of Viṣṇu, it is possible that Viṣṇu is considered as the active power of Śiva and hence these symbols in the hands of the Devī. This surmise is strengthened by the fact that in the Haryardha-mūrti of Śiva, the left half is Viṣṇu and in the Ardhanārīśvara form, Devī forms the left half.

ASPECTS OF PĀRVATĪ

Sapta-mātṛkās:

According to the *Durgāsaptaśatī,* one of the basic texts on the Mother-cult, when Kauśikī Durgā was fighting the demon Raktabīja—whose blood, if spilled, could produce demons similar to him—she manifested out of herself seven emanations. These are usually called the Saptamātṛkas or the 'Seven little Mothers'. They are Brāhmī (or Brahmāṇī) Māheśvarī, Kaumārī, Vaiṣṇavī, Vārāhī, Nārasiṁhī and Aindrī (or Indrāṇī). As their very names indicate, they are the Śaktis of Brahmā, Iśvara, Kumāra (Skanda), Viṣṇu, Varāha, Narasiṁha and Indra. Hence they have the same forms, weapons and vehicles as their lords. Since the Devī, according to the same work, was formed out of the combined energies of all the gods, this theory of the Saptamātṛkas becomes intelligible to us.

Sometimes, Nārasiṁhī is substituted by Cāmuṇḍā (or Cāmuṇḍī). Along with the original deity—called Durgā Mahālakṣmī—they are counted as eight.

Sometimes, an esoteric interpretation is given by the followers of Tantraśāstra, with regard to these seven mātṛkās. Brāhmī, (Fig. 31) according to them, represents the primordial Nāda, the energy in which even the first throb has not yet appeared. This is the unmanifiest sound (Logos), the origin of all creation. It is the same as the substance or energy represented by the Praṇava (Om). When Brāhmī creates the universe, the power of Vaiṣṇavī (Fig. 28) gives it a definite shape. The symmetry, beauty, organisation and order in the universe are the work of Vaiṣṇavī. Māheśvari (Fig. 33) stands for the power that

Fig. 28. Saptamātṛkās-Vaiṣṇavi

gives individuality to the created beings. She resides in the hearts of all and makes them play, like the dolls mounted on a machine. Kaumārī (Fig. 29), the ever youthful deity, represents the ever present force of aspiration of the evolving soul. She is 'Guruguhā, (Guruguha being one of the names of Kumāra or Skanda whose energy she is), the 'Guru' (guide, teacher) in the 'Guhā' (the cave of the heart, the intellect). Vārāhī (Fig. 34) is the all-consuming power

Fig. 29. Kaumārī

Fig. 30. Cāmuṇḍā

of assimilation and enjoyment. Because of her, the living beings get their food and all physical enjoyments. Aindrī or Indrāṇī (Fig. 32) symbolises the terrible power that destroys all that opposes the cosmic law. Cāmuṇḍā (Fig. 30) is the force of concentrated awareness, the power of spiritual awakening in the heart, that devours the ceaseless activity of the immature mind and uplifts it to the highest level. Raktabījāsura is actually the mind, each wave of which gives rise to other waves. Killing of this Raktabīja by Cāmuṇḍā means the destruction of the mental modifications by the awakening of spiritual consciousness.

Fig. 31. Brāhmī

Fig. 32. Aindrī

Fig. 33. Māheśvarī

Fig. 34. Vārāhī

These deities are generally represented as red in colour and with two hands, holding a skull and a lotus. However, since they are Śaktis of the above-mentioned gods, they are shown more often as female replicas of the male deities.

Sometimes each deity is assigned a tree as specially sacred to it. For instance: Udumbara (fig tree) for Kaumārī, Aśvattha (peepal tree) for Vaiṣṇavī and the Karañja (Indian beech) for Vārāhī.

They are usually grouped together with Gaṇeśa and Vīrabhadra flanking on either side and shown on panels in the Śiva temples. Occasionally they have a separate shrine built for them. The order or arrangement varies according to the effect desired. If the safety of the village is desired Brāhmī is installed in the centre. If increase in the population is the goal, Cāmuṇḍā occupies the central place.

Daśamahāvidyās:

Ten aspects of Śakti are sometimes described in Tāntric works. They are termed 'Daśamahāvidyā's. These are the representations of transcendent knowledge and power, the sources of all that is to be known.

The first is Kālī, the goddess of time, that destroys everything. Tārā, the second, is the power of the golden embryo (Hiraṇyagarbha) from which the universe evolves. She also stands for void or the boundless space. The third is Ṣoḍaśī. The word literally means 'one who is sixteen years old.' She is the personification of fullness, of perfection. Bhuvaneśvarī, the fourth Vidyā, represents the forces of the material world, whereas Bhairavī the fifth, stands for desires and temptations leading to destruction and death. Then comes Chinnamastā, the naked deity holding her own severed head in hand and drinking her own blood! She simply represents the continued state of self-sustenance of the created world in which are seen continuous self-destruction and self-renewal, in a cyclic order. Dhūmāvatī, the seventh, personifies the destruction of the world by fire, when only smoke (Dhūma) from its ashes remains. She is sometimes identified with Alakṣmī or Jyeṣṭhādevī. The eighth Vidyā, Bagalā, is a crane-headed goddess, and represents the ugly side of living creatures like jealously, hatred and cruelty. Mātaṅgī, the ninth, is the embodiment of the power of domination. The tenth and the last, Kamalā, is the pure consciousness of the self, bestowing boons and allaying the fears of the supplicants. She is identified with Lakṣmī, the goddess of fortune.

Durgā

Durgā is, perhaps, the most widely worshipped aspect of Śakti. An entire Purāṇa, the *Devibhāgavatam,* has been dedicated to her. Another work, more wellknown than the *Devībhāgavatam,* but containing practically the same material in a concise form, is the *Devīmāhātmyam.* It is also known as the *Durgāsaptaśatī* or *Caṇḍī,* and forms a part of another wellknown Purāṇa, the *Mārkaṇḍeyapurānā.* This work is so highly venerated that every verse of it is considered to be a Mantra (sacred formula) of the Devī and its repetition is believed to confer whatever boons the votary prays for.

Literally 'Durgā' means one who is difficult to approach, or, difficult to know. Being the personification of the totality of the powers of the gods, she is naturally difficult to approach or to know. However, being the Mother of

Durgā

the universe, she is the personification of tender love, when supplicated.

Out of the several aspects of the Śakti put forward by this work, Yoganidrā ('meditation-sleep') comes first. She is the power of sleep, taking recourse to which, Lord Viṣṇu rests between two cycles of creation. She is praised as responsible for the creation, sustenance and withdrawal of the universe. She is the mysterious power, the very personification of knowledge, wisdom and memory. She is pleasant and beautiful. At the same time she is terrible also. This combination of the opposite qualities is possible only for her. She is described as wielding several weapons like the bow, arrow, sword, discus and trident.

The next is Mahiṣāsuramardinī, the deity who took shape as a result of the pooling together of the powers of all the gods, who had been oppressed by the demon Mahiṣāsura. Viṣṇu, Śiva and Brahmā were incensed by hearing the accounts of the misdeeds of Mahiṣāsura and the Devī was born out of their wrath, followed by the wrath of the lesser divinities. The powers of these gods formed her limbs and the exact duplicates of their weapons formed her arsenal. Armed with these formidable weapons and riding on a fierce lion, she challenged Mahiṣāsura and destroyed him along with his army.

This story is followed by an exquisite hymn which combines in itself both poetic excellence and devotional fervour and insight.

She is the power inscrutable, by which the whole universe is permeated and energised. She is the personification of all wealth, power, beauty, as also virtues. She is the embodiment of Yajña (sacrifice), Parāvidyā (the highest knowledge concerning the spirit) as well as Aparāvidyā (knowledge of the secular sciences). It is she who bestows wealth—both material and spiritual—dispels difficulties, and annihilates the evil ones. Her beauty as well as her valour, is incomparable.

The gods could not enjoy their freedom for long. Very soon, they were overpowered by the demons Śumbha and Niśumbha. So they had to run to the Himālayas and supplicate the Devī again. This hymn, wellknown as the 'Aparājitāstotra,' praises her as the 'unconquered.' Her immanence in all the living beings is the main theme of this hymn. The powers and activities of all beings are manifestations of only her power.

In response to this prayer, she manifested herself as Kauśikī Durgā, emanating from the body of Pārvatī, who herself became Kālī the dark one, after this manifestation.

The world-bewitching beauty of Durgā attracted the attention of Śumbha and Niśumbha who sent proposals of marriage through a serf. Unfortunately for them, in a moment of 'weakness and foolishness' she had vowed to marry only him who would vanquish her in battle. All attempts at forcibly dragging her away ended in disaster for the demons. Heads rolled, the intervention of giants like Dhūmralocana, Caṇḍa, Muṇḍa and Rajktabīja not withstanding. Kālī, the fierce black goddess who emerged from the Devī's forehead, beheaded Caṇḍa and Muṇḍa and thus won the name Cāmuṇḍā for herself. Only the battle with Raktabīja was longdrawn needing some special efforts by the Devī since he had the mysterious power to multiply himself through the drops of blood spilled in the battle. Even the Saptamātṛkās who came out of her body to battle, seemed helpless. It was Kālī who managed to spread her extensive tongue and drink away all the blood gushing out of Raktabīja, thus preventing the emergence of more demons and enabling Durgā to exterminate him. The rest was easy. Niśumbha was easily put to death after a mockery of fight. Śumbha being exasperated by now, accused her of taking the help of 'others'! Laughing derisively, the Devī withdrew all her emanations and manifestations into herself, showing that she was always the One without a second. In the ensuing battle, Śumbha the lord of the demons, was easily killed, thus ridding the worlds of a great terror.

This is followed by another piece of prayer, an enchanting poetical hymn, which is as simple as it it elegant. Known as the 'Nārāyaṇīstuti' it starts with fervent appeal to the Mother by the grateful gods to be benign and gracious. The hymn describes her as the mistress and the mother of the whole creation. She is the physical universe. She is the mysterious power of Viṣṇu (Vaiṣṇavīśakti), the original cause, as also the power that deludes beings. It is only by pleasing her that one can hope to get spiritual emancipation. All arts and sciences as also womankind, are her manifestations. She is residing as the intellect in the hearts of human beings. She is the all-devouring time. She is the very personification of all that is good and auspicious. She is ever engaged in protecting her children. The Saptamātṛkās are really her aspects. Kālī, the terrible, with a garland of human skulls round her neck, is also another of her aspects. When pleased, she can remedy all diseases. If displeased, she can destroy all that we love and like to possess. Her votaries are always free from troubles. She is the Supreme Truth described in all the scriptural works.

The work also describes her other manifestations like Vindhyavāsinī (one who lives in the Vindhyas), Raktadantā (of red teeth), Śatākṣī (of hundred eyes), Śākambharī (sustainer of vegetables), Durgā (slayer of demon Durgama) Bhīmā (the terrible) and Bhrāmarī or Bhramarāmbā (having the form of bees).

The Devī as depicted in this work has three major manifestations: Mahākālī, Mahālakṣmi and Mahāsarasvatī. These aspects should not be confused with the Pauraṇic deities, Pārvatī, Lakṣmī and Sarasvatī. They are actually the three major manifestations of the One Supreme Power Maheśvarī, according to the three Guṇas (Tamas, Rajas and Sattva).

The first, Māhākalī, has ten faces and ten feet. She is deep blue in colour, like the gem Nīlamaṇi. She is bedecked with ornaments and wields in her ten hands, the following weapons and objects: sword, discus, mace, arrow, bow, iron club, lance, sling, human head and conch. Being the personification of the Tāmasic aspect of the Devī, she is also the Yoganidrā, who has put Lord Viṣṇu to sleep. It is to her that Brahmā prayed, requesting her to leave Viṣṇu so that the latter could destroy the demons Madhu and Kaiṭabha.

She is the personification of Māyā, the mysterious power of Lord Viṣṇu. Unless she is pleased and voluntarily withdraws, the Lord in us will not awake and destroy the powers of evil which are trying to destroy us. This seems to be the import of the story of Brahmā, Madhu and Kaiṭabha.

Mahālakṣmī, the second, the Rājasic aspect of the Devī is described as red in colour like the coral. She holds in her eighteen hands the rosary, battle-pot, cudgel, lance, sword, shield, conch, bell, wine-cup, trident, noose and the discus Sudarśana. Being 'born' out of the combined wraths and powers of all the gods, she is the personification not only of the powers but also of the will to fight the evil forces. That is why she is shown as red in colour, the colour of blood, the colour of war. It is she who destroyed Mahiṣāsura.

The story of Mahiṣāsura has several implications. Mahiṣāsura, the he-buffalo, represents the jungle law that might is right. He is the ruthless brute force that does not brook any opposition where selfish ends are concerned. And he succeeded even against the gods; but only when they were divided. But he fell before their combined powers and the will to fight, which is exactly what the Devī, Mahiṣāsuramardinī, represents. The lesson of this story at the social level is too obvious to need an explanation. Nor can we ignore its social implications. At the subjective level, Mahiṣāsura stands for ignorance and stubborn egoism. Its subjugation and conquest are possible only when the Sādhaka (spiritual aspirant) pools all his energies together and fights it with a tenacious will. Since God helps him who helps himself, the intervention of the divine power in his favour is always there.

Mahāsarasvatī is the third deity representing the Sāttvic aspect of the Devī. She is bright like the autumn moon and has eight hands in which she holds the bell, trident, ploughshare, conch, pestle, discus, bow and arrow. It is she who manifests out of the physical sheath of Pārvatī and hence known as Kauśikī Durgā. She is the very personification of physical perfection and beauty. She is the power of work, order and organization.

The section dealing with her exploits is the longest. Dhūmralocana, Caṇḍa, Muṇḍa, Raktabīja, Niśumbha and Śumbha are the chief demons destroyed by her. All these demons known as Asuras, are archetypes of highly egoistic people who revel in a life of the pleasures of the body and the sense-organs. Symbolically they represent various stages and states of egoism. If Dhūmralocana ('the smoky-eyed') stands for the grossest state of ignorance and egoism, Raktabīja represents a more subtle state which multiplies itself and our troubles! While Muṇḍa is the low profile of our egoism (muṇḍa=the low), Caṇḍa is the more horrible side of it (caṇḍa=fierce). Śumbha and Niśumbha signify more englightened aspects of egoism (Śumbh= to shine).

Dhūmralocana was destroyed by a Huṅkāra, by a mere frown! Caṇḍa and Muṇḍa were too mean to be handled by the Devī directly. Hence Kālī, the horrible, finished them at her behest. Raktabīja required more skilful handling. The source of his strength was destroyed first before destroying him. As for Niśumbha and Śumbha, the Devī was obliged to give them a straight fight.

Lower states of ignorance and egoism as typified by Dhūmralocana, Caṇḍa and Muṇḍa, should be destroyed by sudden bursts of energy and rough handling. More crafty states which result in endless multiplication of desires—that is what Raktabīja signifies—should be tactfully handled by going to the root, by suppressing them as soon as they arise. 'Enlightened egoiṣm,' if one can use such an expression, which is egoism all the same, needs a straight fight. It may be a long drawn fight and Devī's grace is absolutely necessary for success.

Aspects of Durgā mentioned in the Purāṇas and Āgamas are legion. For instance: Śailaputrī, Kūṣmāṇḍā, Kātyāyanī, Kṣemaṅkarī, Harasidhiḥ, Vanadurgā, Vindhya-vāsinī, Jayadurgā and so on. They are of greater interest in iconography and to the supplicants who can get different types of desires fulfilled by worshipping the different aspects.

Images of Durgā can have four or eight or ten or eighteen or even twenty hands. The eyes are usually three. The hair is dressed up as a crown (called Karaṇḍamukuṭa). She is gorgeously dressed with red cloth and several ornaments. Among the objects held in hand, the more common ones are—conch, discus, trident, bow, arrow, sword, dagger, shield, rosary, winecup and bell. She may be shown as standing on a lotus or on a buffalo's head or as riding a lion.

Lion, the royal beast, her mount, represents the best in animal creation. It can also represent the greed for food, and hence the greed for other objects of enjoyment which inevitably leads to lust. To become divine (Devatva) one should keep one's animal instincts under complete control. This seems to be the lesson we can draw from the picture of the Siṁhavāhinī (the rider of lion).

Kālī

Of all the forms of the Hindu pantheon, that of Kālī is perhaps the most enigmatic to the modern mind. Who will not recoil in horror and disgust form the form of a dark

Fig. 35. Kālī

nude woman wearing an apron of human hands and a garland of human heads, especially if she is also holding a freshly severed human head and the chopper used in the slaughter, dripping with blood? Throughout its history, mankind has been baffled by profound symbology. More so when it does not conform to its own 'sweet and refined' standards. Even when one particular group or cult successfully assimilates it and starts revering it, other groups or cults continue to abhor it. It is natural for one group to abhor the symbols of all others, forgetting conveniently that the 'other groups' are doing the same! The picture of the 'Slain Lamb' or the cultus of the 'Sacred Heart' are just two illustrations to show this. On the other hand, a close look at such symbols will not only dispel our ignorance about them but can also produce positive admiration. Is not the water of the sea, which appears as dark blue or green from a distance, really colourless and transparent when examined at close quarters?

The word 'Kālī' comes from the wellknown word Kāla, time. She is the power of time. Time, as we are all well aware, is all-destroying, all-devouring. That is why the Lord says in the *Gītā* (11.32) that He is time which has grown to infinite proportions and is destroying the worlds. A power that destroys has got to be depicted in terms of awe-inspiring terror.

Let us now turn to the Kālī imagery as normally found in the scriptures, pictures and icons. The background is a cremation ground or a burial ground or a warfield, showing the dead bodies including the mutilated ones. She herself is standing in a challenging posture, on a 'dead' body, which is her own spouse, Śiva himself. If Śiva is pure white, she is deep blue in colour bordering on blackness. She is completely naked, except for an apron of human hands. She is wearing a garland of fifty human heads or skulls. Her luxuriant hair is completely dishevelled. She has three eyes and four hands. In her upper hands she is holding a freshly severed and bleeding human head, as also the sword (or chopper) used in the carnage. The two lower hands are in the Abhaya and Varada Mudrās. Her face is red and the tongue protruding.

The background or the setting is in complete harmony with the theme. The severed head and the sword are graphic representations of destruction that has just taken place.

God is said to have created this universe and then entered into it. (*Taīttirīyopaniṣad* 2.6). So the universe becomes a veil, a cloak for the divinity. When that is destroyed, the divinity remains unveiled. This is the meaning of Kālī being naked. She is hence termed 'Digambarā' ('clad in space'), having the vast limitless space itself as her only vesture.

Being the embodiment of Tamas, the aspect of energy responsible for dispersion ad infinitum producing limitless void, a void that has swallowed up everything, she is black. She represents the state where time, space and causation have disappeared without any trace as it were. Hence she is black.

The hand represents the capacity for work. Hence the apron of severed hands can signify that she is so pleased with the offerings of our works and the fruits thereof that she wears them on her body.

The hand can also stand for kinetic energy. Therefore, severed hands can stand for potential energy, the energy that has stopped all outward manifestation, and yet is tremendously powerful, ready to manifest itself when desired.

The dishevelled hair, for which she is called 'Muktakeśī,' bespeaks her untrammelled freedom.

And then, the garland of skulls or heads which number fifty. They represent the fifty letters of the alphabet, the manifest state of sound, or sound (Śabda) in general, from which the entire creation has proceeded. To show that the manifest creation has been withdrawn, she is wearing the garland on her body. The skulls or severed heads indicate the state of destruction.

Since she is the supreme energy responsible for the dissolution of the created universe, her form as depicted here naturally strikes awe and fear. But then she is the creatrix, the Mother also. Hence she is reassuring her fearstricken children through the Abhaya Mudrā saying, 'Don't be afraid! I am your own dear Mother!' Simultaneously she is also exhibiting her desire to grant boons through the Varada Mudrā.

So far, so good! But what about Śiva Mahādeva being 'trampled' under her feet? According to one of the mythological accounts, Kālī once destroyed all the demons in a battle and then started a terrific dance out of the sheer joy of victory. All the worlds began to tremble and give way under its impact. At the request of all the gods Śiva himself asked her to desist from it. She was too intoxicated to listen. Hence Śiva lay like a corpse among the corpses on which she was dancing in order to absorb its shock into himself. When she stepped upon him she suddenly realised her mistake and put out her tongue in shame!

Śiva Mahādeva is Brahman, the Absolute which is beyond all names, forms and activities. Hence he is shown lying prostrate like a śava, corpse. Kālī represents his śakti or energy. The energy however can never exist apart from its source or act independently of it. It can manifest itself and act only when it is based firmly on the source. It is exactly this that is meant while showing Kālī standing on the chest of Śiva.

From all this, one should not jump to the conclusion that Kālī represents only the destructive aspect of God's power. What exists when time is transcended, the eternal night, of limitless peace and joy, is also Kālī (Mahārātri). Again it is she who prods Śiva Mahādeva into the next cycle of creation. In short, she is the power of God in all His aspects.

Lalitā

Another aspect of the Devī which is more widely worshipped in South India is Lalitā Tripurasundarī. Repetition of the wellknown *Lalitāsahasranāma* and *Triśati**, as also the worship of her emblem, the 'Śrīcakra' are extremely popular. The initiation into her powerful Mantra, the Pañcadaśākṣarī (Mantra of 15 letters) is an esoteric rite. Regular worship of the Śrīcakra is said to yield any result the devotee desires.

---

* Thousand names and three hundred names, respectively of Lalitā Devī.

Fig. 36. Lalitā

If Durgā and Kālī represent the aspects of power of the Goddess, Lalitā represents the aspect of beauty. Hence her form is depicted as extremely beautiful and her worship more refined.

According to the *Lalitopākhyāna* of the *Brahmāṇḍa Purāṇa*, Lalitā Devī manifested herself in the midst of a disc of extreme brilliance, that arose from the sacrificial pit when Indra was performing a sacrifice in honour of her. At the behest of the gods assembled there, she chose to wed Kāmeśvara (Lord Śiva). She destroyed the demon Bhaṇḍāsura and annihilated his city, the Śoṇitapura. Viśvakarmā, the engineer of the gods, built a gorgeous city 'Śrīpura' on the mountain Meru, for her sake, where, along with her spose Śiva Kāmeśvara, she is residing eternally. The Śrīcakra actually represents the Devī in this Śrīpura.

Bhaṇḍāsura, the shameless demon, living in the Soṇitapura, the city of blood and flesh, is actually the ego which makes the soul identify itself with the body and estrange itself from all the divine forces. When the Devī, who is the embodiment of God's power and grace, 'kills' it, she is actually liberating it from its stifling limitations.

Lalitā is usually depicted as slightly red in colour (as that of the dawn) and extraordinarily beautiful. In her four hands she is holding a bow of sugarcane, arrows, the goad (Aṅkuśa) and the noose (Pāśa). Sometimes she is shown holding a wine cup made of diamond. One of her feet, usually the left, is shown resting on a pedestal, also of diamond.

The bow made of sugarcane actually represents the mind. It is through the mind that we experience all joy.

Hence it is described as made of sugarcane. The bow is the instrument for discharging the arrows. The mind is the instrument by which the sense organs are 'shot' towards the sense-objects. Hence it is described as a bow. The arrows are the Pañca-tanmātras, the five subtle elements of Ākāśa (ether), Vāyu (air), Agni (fire), Āpas (water), Pṛthivī (earth). The sense organs like the eye and the ear, are products of these subtle elements and are discharged like arrows, through the mind, towards the sense-objects. Hence the subtle elements are described as the arrows in her hand. She is the power that energises and controls our minds and sense organs. This is the underlying idea. The Pāśa (noose) is actually Rāga (attachment) which binds. The Aṅkuśa (goad) is Krodha (anger, aversion) which hurts. The power that animates our attachments and aversions is also hers. If we forget her, she can bind us with Rāgapāśa, and pierce us with the Krodhāṅkuśa. If we take refuge in her, she can withdraw them into her hands and thereby free us from their torment.

An account of Lalitā cannot be complete without a few words of description of the Śrīcakra. The Śrīcakra is essentially a yantra.* the form and pattern of the deity. It is

*Practically every deity of the Hindu pantheon has three modes of expression or manifestation: (a) the Mūrti, the three-dimensional form which can be sculptured; (b) the Yantra, a two-dimensional or geometric pattern which can be drawn; and (c) the Mantra, the sound form or the thought form, which can be uttered in contemplation. The 'Mūrti' is usually described in the appropriate Dhyānaśloka (verse chanted at the beginning of meditation, to call up the form of the deity into the mind) and dealt with in greater detail in the iconographical works.

a rather complicated geometrical figure of forty three triangles formed by the intersection of nine triangles, of which five have their apexes downward and the other four upward. This is surrounded by concentric circles with eight and then sixteen lotus petals. The whole figure is skirted by a square of three lines with openings in the middle of each side. There is a dot in the centre of the entire diagram.

This dot represents the combination of Śiva and Śakti, as also the first throb, which gradually gathers momentum and gets concentrated into a polarisation of Śiva and Śakti, but continuing to keep the original Śiva-Śakti combination also. The process repeats continuously resulting in various levels of creation, which are depicted by the different triangles and the lotus petals.

The Śrīcakra can be used for permanent worship either in the form of a Yantra (two dimensional engraved figure) or in the form of Meru (three dimensional embossed figure).

The Yantra and Mantra are described in Tāntric works. The Mantra, when received from a competent Guru and repeated with intense faith and devotion, is capable of revealing the form of the deity by setting up appropriate vibrations in the ākāśa (ether) which pervades everything including one's own body and mind. The yantra, the geometrical abode of the deity, when drawn properly (using the dot, the straight line, the triangle, the circle, the segment and so on), and installed, gets charged as it were, binding the contemplated deity to itself. Though the Śrīcakra is comparatively more well-known, there are a good number of other Yantras or Cakras which are still very much in vogue.

OTHER ASPECTS OF PĀRVATĪ

As already mentioned, the number of aspects, both major and minor, of Devī or Śakti (i.e., Pārvatī) is too numerous to deal with in a small book like this. Apart from the three major ones dealt with so far, a few others which are more commonly known will now be dealt with very briefly.

Annapūrṇā: 'The possessor and giver of food.' Pārvatī got this name since she served food to Śiva when he was roaming about as a mendicant. She is shown serving food from a vessel of ruby. Her worship ensures that the household will never lack food. Her temple at Kāśī is very famous.

Aparājitā: 'The Invincible.' It is actually one of the names of Durgā and the wellknown series of verses in the Caṇḍī ending with the words 'namas tasyai' are called 'Aparājitāstotra'.

Bālā: 'The Child.' Considered to be the daughter of Lalitā and always nine years old, she is said to have destroyed the thirty sons of Bhaṇḍāsura.

Bhadrakālī: One of the several aspects of Mahākālī. She is said to have sprung from Umā's wrath when Dakṣa insulted Śiva and fought along with Vīrabhadra to destroy Dakṣa's sacrifice.

Bhūtamātā: 'The Mother of goblins.' She resides under the Aśvattha (pipal) tree and has a host of demons, goblins and demigods as her retinue.

Cāmuṇḍā: Same as Kālī. She got this name since she killed Caṇḍa and Muṇḍa in the battle against Śumbha and

Niśumbha. She is sometimes included under the Saptamātṛkās.

Gāyatrī, Sāvitrī and Sarasvatī: These three goddesses represent the presiding deities of the famous Gāyatrī Mantra chanted three times a day. Gāyatrī is the presiding deity of the morning prayer, rules over the *Ṛgveda* and the Gārhapatya fire.* She has four faces, four or ten arms and rides on a swan. Sāvitrī presides over the noon prayer, rules over the *Yajurveda* and the Dakṣiṇā fire. She has four faces, twelve eyes, four arms and rides on a bull. Sarasvatī is the deity presiding over the evening prayer, rules over the *Sāmaveda* and the Āhavanīya fire. She has one face and four arms, and rides over Garuḍa.

Indrākṣī: "One whose eyes are similar to Indra's." She is the aspect of Devī specially worshipped by Indra as also the Apsara women (heavenly damsels). She is richly decorated and holds the Vajrāyudha. If she is pleased by hymns, she can cure even incurable diseases.

Jagad-dhātrī: 'One who sustains the world.' Another aspect of the Devī which is more common in Bengal. She has four arms carrying the conch, discus, bow and arrow and rides on a lion.

Kāmeśvarī: 'The Mistress of desire.' Since Lord Śiva destroyed Kāma, the god of lust, he is known as Kāmeśvara, 'One who is the lord of lust or desire.' The Devī being his consort, is known as Kāmeśvarī. This

---

* Every householder of the first three Varṇas was expected to keep five or three sacred fires in his house, for the performance of Vedic rituals.

is actually one of the names of Lalitā. She can fulfil any of our desires for which we supplicate her.

Kātyāyanī: Since the Devī was once born as the daughter of a sage Kata by name, she is known as Kātyāyanī. She is the totality of the powers of the Hindu Trinity. Her description practically tallies with that of Durgā as Mahiṣāsuramardinī.

Manonmanī: 'One who lifts the mind up to the highest state of Yoga.' She is the Śakti established in the psychic centre in the top of the head, just below the Brahmarandhra. She is pictured as blue or black in complexion and carries a skull-cup as also a sword. When she is pleased by the devoted prayers of her votaries, she can grant wealth and terrify their enemies.

Rājarājeśvarī: 'One who rules over the king of kings.' The Devī is the mistress of even Brahmā, Viṣṇu and Maheśvara as also Kubera (the lord of wealth), who are known as 'king of kings'. She is an aspect of Lalitā.

Śivadūtī: In her battle against Śumbha and Niśumbha, the Devī once sent her spouse Śiva himself as a messenger (Dūta) to them. Hence she came to be known as Śivadūtī, 'one who has Śiva himself as her messenger.' Iconographically she is sometimes shown like Kālī and sometimes like Durgā.

9

MINOR DEITIES

Gaṇapati

Gaṇapati or Gaṇeśa, also known as Vināyaka, is perhaps, the most popular of the Hindu deities worshipped by all sections of the Hindus. No undertaking, whether sacred or secular, can get started without first honouring and worshipping him. This is understandable and highly desirable, since he is said to be the lord of obstacles (Vighneśvara or Vighnarāja). However, what is not understandable and certainly not very agreeable is his repulsive origin and grotesque form! Even for those who admire Lord Śiva's skill in the surgical art of head-transplantation, it becomes rather difficult to admire the end product! Once we successfully manage to delve into the mysteries of this symbolism our repugnance will give rise to respect and respect to reverence and worship.

Notwithstanding the fact that the Gaṇapati referred to in the famous Ṛgvedic mantras, 'gaṇānāṁ gaṇapatiṁ havāmahe...' (2.23.1) and 'viṣu sīda gaṇapate...' (10.112. 9) and the Gaṇapati we worship today are strangers to each other, all unbiased scholars agree that the seeds of the Gaṇapati concept are already there in the *Ṛgveda* itself. In the subsequent centuries, this concept has passed through the mills of the epics and the Purāṇas to produce the Gaṇapati as we know him today. In any community, the development of the concept of God and the modes of His worship are as much the products of geographical, historical and cultural factors as of mystic experience and spiritual realizations of the highly evolved persons. It is quite reasonable to suppose that the 'Gaṇapati-Brahmaṇaspati' of the Ṛgveda gradually got metamorphosed into the deity, 'Gajavadana-Gaṇeśa-Vighneśvara.'

The Ṛgvedic deity 'Gaṇapati-Brahmaṇaspati'—also called as Bṛhaspati and Vācaspati—manifests himself through a vast mass of light. He is golden-red in colour.

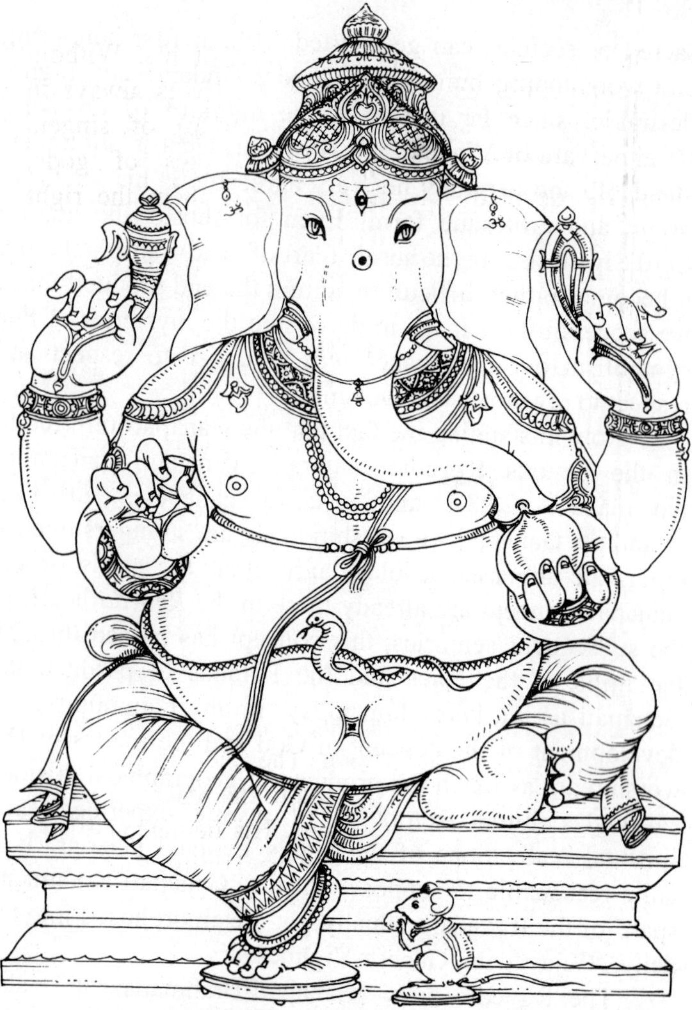

Fig. 37. Gaṇapati

The battle axe is an important weapon of his. Without his grace no religious rite can succeed. He is always in the company of a group (gaṇa=a group) of singers and dancers. He vanquishes the enemies of gods, protects the devoted votaries and shows them the right way of life.

Another class of Ṛgvedic deities, known as the Maruts or Marud-gaṇa, described as the children of Rudra, also have similar characteristics. In addition, they can be malevolent towards those who antagonise them and can cause destruction like the wild elephants. They can put obstacles in the path of men if displeased and remove them when pleased. They are independent, not subject to any one's sovereignty (Arājana=Vināyaka).

A perusal of these two descriptions will perforce lead us to the obvious conclusion that Gaṇapati is the metamorphosed form of the Bṛhaspati-Marudgaṇa deities. There is nothing strange in this, especially if we can recognize the transformations that have taken place among the various Vedic deities, as they were gradually absorbed among the gods of the later Hindu pantheon. The once all-important and all-powerful Indra was demoted to the rank of a minor deity ruling over one of the quarters. His lieutenant Viṣṇu was elevated to the central place in the Trinity. Rudra, the terrible, became Śiva the auspicious. Many other deities like Dyaus, Aryaman and Pūṣan were quietly despatched into oblivion!

Despite the fact that Gaṇapati is a highly venerated and all-important deity, his 'head' has often been a mystery for others. No doubt, our Purāṇas have easily 'solved' this problem, each in its own way. But this has satisfied neither the layman nor the scholar.

It will be extremely interesting to bring together, though in brief, all the stories about the origin of this wondrous deity:

(1) At the request of the gods who wanted a deity capable of removing all obstacles from their path of action and fulfilment, Śiva himself was born of the womb of Pārvatī as Gajānana.

(2) Once Pārvatī, just for fun, prepared an image of a child with an elephant's head, out of the unguents smeared over her body and threw it into the river Gaṅgā. It came to life. Both Gaṅgā, the guardian deity of the river and Pārvatī, addressed the boy as their child. Hence he is known as Dvaimātura, 'one who has two mothers'.

(3) Pārvatī prepared the image of a child out of the scurf from her body, endowed him with life and ordered him to stand guard before her house. When Siva wanted to enter the house he was rudely prevented by this new gatekeeper. Śiva became 'Rudra' and got him beheaded. Seeing that Pārvatī was inconsolable owing to this tragedy that befell her 'son' and not finding the head of the body anywhere—meanwhile one of the goblins of Śiva had gourmandized it!—he got an elephant's head, grafted it on to the body of the boy and gave him life. To make amends for his 'mistake', Siva appointed this new-found son as the head of all his retinues, who thus became 'Gaṇapati'.

(4) He sprang from Śiva's countenance which represents the principle of ether (Ākāśatattva). His captivating

splendour made Pārvatī react angrily and curse him, resulting in his uncouth form!

(5) Gaṇeśa was originally Kṛṣṇa himself in the human form. When Śani, the malevolent planet spirit gazed at him, his head got separated and flew to Goloka, the world of Kṛṣṇa. The head of an elephant was subsequently grafted on the body of the child.

Equally interesting are the other myths about his adventures: He lost one of his tusks in a fight with Paraśurāma, which he successfully used as a stylus to write the epic *Mahābhārata* dictated by the sage Vyāsa. He tactfully won the race against his brother Skanda by circumambulating his parents and declaring that it was equivalent to going round the worlds. He thus won the hands of two damsels Ṛddhi and Siddhi. He cursed the moon to wax and wane, since the latter derisively laughed at him when he was trying to refill his burst belly with the sweets that had spilled out. He vanquished the demon Vighnāsura and successfully brought him under his subjugation.

There is no gainsaying the possibilities of man developing the concept of God and faith in Him as a result of his experiences through the various vicissitudes of life which prove his helplessness. He often disposes, what he proposes. Such a God must needs be allpowerful. If he is pleased, all the obstacles in our path will be removed. If displeased He may thwart our efforts and make them infructuous. Hence the paramount need to appease Him and please Him.

What could be the form of this almighty God? For a simple aboriginal living in a group (=Gaṇa) near a forest or a mountain, the mighty elephant might have provided the clue. This might have led to the worship of an elephant-like God. He being the Pati (=Lord) of the Gaṇa (clan or group) might have obtained the name Gaṇapati. As the group became more refined and cultured, this Elephant God might have been transformed into the present form.

However plausible or attractive this hypothesis may be, it is at best a guesswork, if not an invention! Since Gaṇapati had gained *de facto* recognition in the hearts of millions of votaries, over several centuries, the Purāṇas rightly struggled to make it *de jure!* True, they have given very confusing accounts. Nevertheless they have succeeded in fusing together the votaries by giving them a scriptural or authoritative base. There is certainly no contradiction or confusion in the accounts as far as the worship and its result are concerned.

It is a favourite pastime of some western scholars and their Indian counterparts to 'discover' a Draviḍian base for many interesting developments in our cultural and religious life and then to 'unearth' the further fact of the white-skinned Āryan 'conquerors' graciously and condescendingly absorbing these, tactfully elevating the same to 'higher' levels all the while. This has naturally led to a vigorous reaction and these 'reactionaries' go the whole hog to 'prove' it the other way round! When our Gaṇapati is caught in the web of such controversies one may be driven to the ridiculous conclusion that he is not an Āryan deity at all, but, most probably, imported from Mongolia! It is therefore better to play safe, rescue our deity from embarrassing situations and get the best out of him for our spiritual life.

The most commonly accepted form of Gaṇapati depicts him as red in colour and in a human body with an elephant's head. Out of the two tusks, one is broken. He has four arms. Two of the arms hold the Pāśa (noose) and Aṅkuśa (goad). The other two are held in the Abhaya and Varada Mudrās. The belly is of generous proportions and is decorated with a snake-belt. There is also a Yajñopavita (sacred Brahminical thread), either of thread or of serpent. He may be seated in Padmāsana (lotus-posture). When the belly does not permit this, the right leg may be shown bent and resting on the seat.

Apart from beautiful robes and ornaments, he wears a lovely carved crown.

The trunk may be turned to the left or to the right.

He is normally seen helping himself to liberal quantities of Modaka (a kind of sweet).

A mouse, of ridiculously small proportions, is seen near him, nibbling at his share of the sweets, hoping perhaps, to gain enough strength to carry his master!

A third eye may sometimes be added on the forehead, in the centre of the eyebrows. The number of heads may be raised to five. The arms may vary from two to ten. Lotus, pomegranate, water-vessel, battle-axe, lute, broken tusk, sugarcane, ears of paddy, bow and arrow, thunderbolt, rosary, book—these are some of the other objects shown in the hands. His Śakti is often shown with him as sitting on his lap. Sometimes two Śaktis, Ṛddhi* and Siddhi, are also shown.

---

* According to some accounts, she is replaced by Buddhi.

Let us now make an attempt at unravelling this symbology.

'Gaṇa' means category. Everything that we perceive through our senses or grasp through our mind can be expressed in terms of kind, of category. The principle from which all such categories have manifested themselves is Gaṇapati, the Lord of categories. In effect, it means the origin of the whole creation, God Himself.

A common Sanskrit word to denote the elephant is 'Gaja'. Hence the name Gajānana or Gajamukha ('elephant-faced') for Gaṇapati. But the word 'Gaja' has a much deeper connotation. 'Ga' indicates 'Gati,' the final goal towards which the entire creation is moving, whether knowingly or unknowingly. 'Ja' stands for 'Janma,' birth or origin. Hence 'Gaja' signifies God from whom the worlds have come out and towards whom they are progressing, to be ultimately dissolved in Him. The elephant head is thus purely symbolical and points to this truth.

Another factor we observe in creation is its two-fold manifestation as the microcosm (Sūkṣmāṇḍa) and the Macrocosm (Brahmāṇḍa). Each is a replica of the other. They are one in two and two in one. The elephant head stands for the macrocosm and the human body for the microcosm. The two form one unit. Since the macrocosm is the goal of the microcosm, the elephant part has been given greater prominence by making it the head.

Perhaps, the boldest statement concerning philosophical truths ever made is contained in that pithy saying of the *Chāndogya Upanisad*: 'tat-tvam-asi,' 'That thou art.' It simply means: 'You, the apparently limited individual, are, in essence, the Cosmic Truth, the Absolute.' The elephant-human form of Gaṇapati is the iconographical representation of this great Vedāntic dictum. The elephant stands for the cosmic whereas the human stands for the individual. The single image reflects their identity.

Among the various myths that deal with Gaṇapati's origin, the one that attributes it to the scurf or dirt taken out of her body by Pārvatī seems to be the most widely known, and considered as odd and odious. It is therefore worthwhile to delve a little deeper into this mystery.

One of the epithets by which Gaṇapati is well known and worshipped is 'Vighneśvara' or 'Vighnarāja' ('The Lord of obstacles'). He is the lord of all that obstructs or restricts, hinders or prevents. With the various grades and shades of the powers of obstruction under his control, he can create a hell of trouble for us if he wants! In fact, according to the mythological accounts, the very purpose of his creation was to obstruct the progress in the path of perfection!

How does he do it? If he is not appeased by proper worship, all undertakings, whether sacred or secular, will meet with so many obstacles that they will simply peter out. This is to show that nothing can succeed without his grace. If he is pleased by worship and service, he will tempt his votaries with success and prosperity (Siddhi and Ṛddhi) the very taste of which can gradually lead them away from the spiritual path. Why does he do it? To test them thoroughly before conferring upon them the greatest spiritual boon of Mokṣa. Being the master of all arts and sciences, and the repository of all knowledge, he can easily confer success or perfection in any of these. However, he is unwilling to give spiritual knowledge leading to the highest spiritual experience, lest it should appear easy of achievement in the eyes of men. Hence the severity of the test. The path of the good is fraught with innumerable obstacles, 'śreyāṁsi bahuvighnāni.' Only the very best of heroes, who can brave the roughest of weathers, deserve to be blessed with it. Human beings by nature are inclined towards the enjoyments of the flesh and intoxications of power and pelf. It is only one in a million that turns towards God. Among many such souls, very few survive the struggles and reach the goal. (*vide Gītā 7.3*)

When compared to the highest spiritual wisdom, which alone is really worth striving for, even Ṛddhi and Siddhi (success and prosperity) are like impurities, Mala, as it were. Since Gaṇapati's consorts are Ṛddhi and Siddhi (personifications of the powers of success and prosperity), he, their spouse, has been described as created out of Pārvatī's bodily scurf.

Again, the word 'Mala' need not have any odium about it. If Śiva represents Paramapuruṣa, the Supreme Person, Pārvatī stands for Paramā Prakṛti, Nature Supreme, considered as His power, inseparable from Him. She is, in the language of philosophy, Māyā-prakṛti, comprising the three Guṇas—Sattva, Rajas and Tamas. Sattva is stated to be pure and, as compared to it, Rajas and Tamas are said to be 'impure'. Since creation is impossible out of pure Sattva, even as pure gold does not lend itself to be shaped into ornaments unless mixed with baser metals, it has got to be mixed with Rajas and Tamas to effect it. This seems to be the import of the story of the 'impure' substances being used by Mother Pārvatī to shape Gaṇapatī.

Let us now try to interpret the other factors involved in the symbology of this god. His ears are large, large enough to listen to the supplications of everyone, but, like the winnowing basket, are capable of sifting what is good for the supplicant from what is not. Out of the two tusks, the one that is whole stands for the Truth, the One without a second. The broken tusk, which is imperfect, stands for the manifest world, which appears to be imperfect because of the inherent incongruities. However, the manifest universe and the unmanifest unity are both attributes of the same Absolute. The bent trunk is a representation of Oṅkāra or Praṇava which, being the symbol of Brahman, the Absolute, is declaring as it were that Gaṇapati is Brahman Itself. His large belly indicates that all the created worlds are contained in him.

The Pāśa (noose) stands for Rāga (attachment), and the Aṅkuśa (goad) for Krodha (anger). Like the noose, attachment binds us. Anger hurts us like the goad. If God is displeased with us, our attachments and anger will increase, making us miserable. The only way of escaping from the tyranny of these is to take refuge in God. Or it can mean that it is far safer for us to surrender our attachment and anger to Him. When they are in His hands, we are safe!

How we wish that Lord Gaṇapati had chosen a big bandicoot as his mount. The fact, however, is otherwise and that privilege has been conferred on a small mouse!

The word Mūṣaka (=mouse) is derived from the root 'muṣ' which means 'to steal'. A mouse stealthily enters into things and destroys them from within. Similarly egoism enters unnoticed, into our minds and quietly destroys all our undertakings. Only when it is controlled by divine wisdom, it can be harnessed to useful channels. Or, the mouse that steals, can represent love that steals the human hearts. As long as human love is kept at the low level, it can create havoc. Once it is directed towards the Divine, it elevates us. The mouse that is wont to see the inside of all things can stand for the incisive intellect. Since Gaṇapati is the lord of the intellect, it is but meet that he has chosen it as his vehicle.

ICONS OF GAṆAPATI

There are several varieties of Gaṇapati icons available in our temples and archaelogical monuments. Whether the number is 71,50,31, or 21, it is certain that there are several aspects of this deity. Only a few of them can be dealt with here.

'Bālagaṇapati' and 'Taruṇagaṇapati' images depict him as a child and a young man, respectively. 'Vināyaka' is shown with four arms holding the broken tusk, goad, noose and rosary. He holds the sweet modaka in his trunk. He may be standing or seated. 'Herambagaṇapati' has five heads, ten hands, three eyes in each face and rides on a lion. 'Vīravighneśa' exhibits the martial spirit with several weapons held in his ten hands. 'Śaktigaṇapati,' several varieties of which are described in the Tantras, is shown with his Śakti, called variously as Lakṣmī, Ṛddhi, Siddhi,

Puṣṭi and so on. Worship of this aspect is said to confer special powers or grant the desired fruits quickly.

One of the varieties of this 'Śaktigaṇapati' is called 'Ucchiṣṭagaṇapati,' the Gaṇapati associated with unclean things like orts, whose worship belongs to Vāmācāra ('the left-handed path,' i.e., the heterodox and unclean path) and said to give quick results. There is nothing to dread or recoil in this concept. Dirty things are as much a part of nature as clean things. But, do not scavengers and doctors handle them in a hygienic way and serve the people? Are not all people obliged to be scavengers in varying degrees? Why not do it religiously, as an act of service and worship? Nature converts clean things into unclean things and vice versa. Making Gaṇapati preside over it and handle dirt scientifically and religiously can also be a spiritual discipline. This seems to be the philosophy behind this concept.

'Nṛttagaṇapati' is a beautiful image showing him as dancing. It seems once Brahmā met Gaṇapati and bowed down to him with great devotion and reverence. Being pleased with this Gaṇapati started dancing gracefully. That is why Gaṇapati is declared to be the master of the arts of music and dancing.

'Varasiddhi Vināyaka' is the aspect worshipped during the famous Gaṇeśa Caturthī festival. He is said to be a celibate.

Gaṇapati is sometimes depicted as a Śakti (female deity) under the names of Gaṇeśānī, Vināyakī, Śūrpakarṇī, Lambamekhalā and so on.

Gaṇapati is worshipped not only in images but also in Liṅgas, Śālagrāmas, Yantras (geometrical diagrams) and

Kalaśas (pots of water). Gaṇapati Śalagrāmas however, are very rare. The Svastika is also accepted as a graphic symbol of Gaṇapati.

Temples and shrines dedicated to Gaṇapati are very numerous. They are spread all over the country. He appears in the campuses of temples of most other deities also.

Subrahmaṇya

If Gaṇapati is universally revered by almost all the Hindus, Buddhists and Jains, and has even succeeded in going abroad to many countries of South East Asia, China, Japan and Afghanistan, Subrahmaṇya his brother, has somehow remained confined to South India. Historically speaking, he is a much older deity, being mentioned in stone inscriptions and shown on coins (1st cent. to 5th cent. A.D.), and was well-known in North India. The sixth day of a lunar month (ṣaṣṭhī) is considered sacred to him (as with serpent deities). He is said to have been married to a forest maid Vaḷḷi-amma. The peacock is his carrier mount. His temples are usually found on hill-tops. All these factors may indicate that he was a sylvan deity connected with serpent-worship and treeworship, and hence was more popular among the people of lower strata in the society. Now, however, all sections of Hinduism have accepted him and they venerate him.

He is said to have been born of Śiva from Pārvatī, to destroy the demon Tārakāsura. Before conceiving him, even these Parents of the World had to perform severe Tapas or austerities! This teaches the world, of the great need for Tapas on the part of the parents desirous of

Fig. 38. Subrahmaṇya

excellence of offspring. He is stated to have been born in a forest of arrow-like grass (hence the name Śaravaṇabhava) and reared by the six divine mothers of the constellation Kṛttikā (Pleiades). Hence the names 'Kārttikeya' and 'Ṣaṇmātura'. It seems he assumed six faces to suckle the milk of the six mothers and so got the appellation 'Ṣaḍānana or Ṣaṇmukha'. He was appointed the commander-in-chief of the gods and thus became 'Devasenāpati'. With his matchless weapon, the Śakti or lance, shining brilliantly like fire, he easily destroyed Tārakāsura, thus becoming 'Śaktidhara' and 'Tārakāri'. Being very young and virile he is 'Kumāra' or 'Sanatkumāra.' A forceful attacker in war, he is known as 'Skanda'. 'Skanda' also means one who has accumulated the power of chastity. He likes holy people (Brāhmaṇas) and is always good to them. Hence he is 'Subrahmaṇya'. Once he broke down the Krauñca-parvata (a mountain), earning the name Krauñcabhettā. At another time he exposed Brahmā's ignorance of the Vedas and hence got the name Brahma-Śāstā. His other names are Guha (the secret one), Gāṅgeya (son of Gaṅgā) and Svāmi-nātha (the preceptor of his own father).

In icons, he is shown as a boy either with one head and two arms or with six heads and twelve arms. His lance and his peacock are also prominently displayed. A fowl adorns his banner.

Subrahmaṇya, the son of Śiva and Śakti, represents the highest state to which a spiritual aspirant can evolve. Etymologically the word 'Subrahmaṇya' means 'one who tends the spiritual growth of the aspirants'. It is only he who has reached the summit of spiritual perfection in this life, that is capable of tending the spiritual growth of others. Mythology describes him as the Son of God begotten to save the world from the tyranny of the fiend Tārakāsura. This is more true in the spiritual sense.

Subrahmaṇya, the Ṣaṇmukha, is depicted with six heads and twelve hands, all of them being attached to one trunk resting on two feet.

Of course, even a boy knows that biologically this is impossible even as an angel with wings is! But a concept like this can be conceded if it fits into useful philosophical postulations. His six heads represent the five sense organs and the mind, which co-ordinates their activities. When these are controlled, refined and sublimated, man becomes a superman. This is the implication of the symbology.

According to Yoga psychology, there are six centres of psychic energy, of consciousness, in the human body, designated as Cakras. They are: Mūlādhāra (at the anus), Svādhiṣṭhāna (at the root of the sex organ), maṇipūra (at the navel) Anāhata (at the region of the heart), Viśuddha (at the throat) Ājñā (between the eyebrows) and Sahasrāra at the top of the head which is the destination for this energy. When the Yogi successfully raises his psychic energy to this topmost centre he has a vision of Śiva-Śakti.

Though it is the same energy that flows through all the six centres, in the case of an ordinary being it is concentrated in the three lowest centres. In a perfect being the flow is so refined and uniform, that practically all the centres have been elevated to the highest level. Subrahmaṇya represents this perfected state of spiritual consciousness.

Man has only two hands. But, his superior intellect has enabled him to invent so many tools and instruments through which he can accomplish manual tasks, even simultaneously. Subrahmaṇya with his twelve hands, symbolically represents this power and capacity of man.

The combination of the six heads and twelve hands teaches us that the ideal of humanity is the perfected being who is not only a great Yogi but also a great worker!

Subrahmaṇya has two consorts: Vaḷḷi and Devasenā. The former is the daughter of a humble chieftain of a race given to agriculture and woodcraft. The latter is the daughter of Indra, the king of gods. This is just to show that God does not make any distinction between the humble folk and the elite. He loves both equally. Alternatively, this can also mean that the true leader of a society will espouse agriculture and industry on the one hand, and the armed forces on the other, in order to develop the society as also to protect it.

The lance of dazzling brightness, is the weapon with which this Devasenāpati vanquished many an enemy. It actually stands for knowledge and wisdom with which all the ugly demons of ignorance can be destroyed.

The peacock is his mount. It is shown as belabouring a snake with one of its legs. The snake stands for time. The peacock that kills it stands for what is opposed to it. By riding the peacock he is showing that he is beyond what is within time and outside it. He is beyond all dualities.

If the snake represents lust, as it often does in the symbology of psychology, the peacock signifies the power of celibacy. As Skanda, he is the very personification of the powers of chastity and hence is shown as riding on the peacock.

Lastly, the peacock, with its beautiful plumage, represents creation in all its glory. Hence he that rides it is the Supreme Lord, the master of creation.

Śāstā, Ārya or Hariharaputra

The Hindu genius has the peculiar virtue of reconciling the irreconcilables. At a time when the Śaivas and Vaiṣṇavas were at loggerheads, the story in the *Bhāgavata* (8.12), of Śiva being enraptured by the voluptuous beauty of (Viṣṇu as) Mohinī, the enchantress, must have come in very handy. By taking it to the logical conclusion it produced the wonderful deity Hariharaputra or Śāstā, more commonly known as 'Ayyappan' (a corrupted form of Ārya). Whatever he might have been in the beginning, he was certainly not a compromise candidate tolerated by both the groups, but Supreme God Himself, highly venerated by both.

Mythological accounts, of course, have their own story to tell. After the death of Mahiṣāsura at the hands of Durgā, his spouse Mahiṣī performed severe austerities to please Brahmā. She succeeded in getting the boon that she could not be killed by Śiva or Viṣṇu. This newfound strength of Mahiṣī posed a formidable challenge to the gods and the world. Śiva and Viṣṇu, who could not singly vanquish her, hit upon the plan of coming together to create her destroyer. The child thus created was found by King Rājaśekhara of Panthalam in Kerala who named it as Maṇikaṇṭhan and brought it up as his own son, since he had

Fig. 39. Śāstā, Ārya or Hariharaputra

no offspring. When Maṇikaṇṭhan was twelve years old, he killed Mahiṣī and brought leopardesses to his father's palace since their milk was needed to cure the 'headache' of the queen. Meanwhile to the king had been revealed the secret of Maṇikaṇṭhan being God Himself. Adored by the king Maṇikaṇṭhan disappeared, after instructing him to build a temple at the place where his arrow would land. That was the summit of the hill Śabarīmalai. The temple is said to have been built by Viśvakarmā and the image prepared and installed by Paraśurāma. The place attracts millions of pilgrims even now.

The word 'Śāstā' means one who controls and rules over the whole world. Mahāśāstā and Dharmaśāstā are the other names by which the deity is known. 'Sāstā' is one of the names of Buddha. The deity is said to ride on a white elephant called Yogi. He is also described as the protector of Dharma. Hence some scholars opine that Dharma-Śāstā may be Buddha absorbed into the Hindu pantheon by the South Indian Hindus.

The image of Śāstā has four arms, three eyes and a peaceful countenance, and is seated in Padmāsana. Two of the hands carry the sword and the shield and the other two exhibit the Abhaya and Varada Mudrās.

According to another version, the image should have only two hands and two eyes, and should be seated with the legs folded. It should be bedecked with ornaments and have the Yajñopavīta. A crooked stick, fruits and tender leaves of plants are sometimes shown in his hands. A Vajradaṇḍa is also shown occasionally.

Images in the standing posture are also seen to exist, though rare.

The ritual pilgrimage to the shrine of Śri Ayyappan at Śabarīmalai is considered to be extremely auspicious and meritorious. The pilgrimage itself has to be preceded by forty-one days of austerity during which period strict celibacy is to be observed as also restrictions regarding food, speech and sleep.

NAVAGRAHAS

For thousands of years, people all over the world have believed in the influence of the planets on human life and history. Logically speaking, the creation of the planets precedes that of the living beings. Hence, some sort of cause and effect relation must subsist between these two. This seems to be the basis for this belief.

The Navagrahas or the nine planets are regarded by the Hindus as of the greatest astrological significance and are believed to influence the life of the individual as also the course of history.

As per the traditional list, the nine planets are Ravi or Sūrya (sun), Soma or Candra (moon), Maṅgala, Kuja or Aṅgāraka (Mars), Budha (Mercury), Bṛhaspati or Guru (Jupiter), Śukra (Venus), Śani (Saturn), Rāhu and Ketu. The seven days of the week have derived their names from the first seven planets. Rāhu and Ketu are not planets but ascending and descending nodes of the moon. Sometimes Ketu is depicted as the personification of comets and meteors.

Śani, Rāhu and Ketu are considered inauspicious, even positively maleficent, and responsible for children's diseases. Hence they need to be propitiated.

Fig. 40. Sūrya

The nine planets are invariably found in every Śaiva temple in South India. In many North Indian temples they

Fig. 41. Soma

are depicted on the lintels of doors, to protect the temple and all those who enter it. They may also be housed in a separate Maṇḍapa (a small pavilion) or at least a platform where the images of these nine Grahas are installed in such

Fig. 42. Maṅgala

a way that no two of them will face each other. It is sometimes stated that the images of the planets are set up in the

Fig. 43. Budha

temples in the order in which they are in zodiacal circle at the time of construction of the temple.

Fig. 44. Guru

The image of Sūrya must always be placed in the centre of the planets, facing east, with the other Grahas fixed round him, each in a specified direction. He has two hands, holding a lotus in each. His chariot has one wheel, is

Fig. 45. Śukra

drawn by seven horses and has Aruṇa (deity of the dawn) as the charioteer.

Fig. 46. Śani

Fig. 47. Rāhu

Fig. 48. Ketu

Soma or Candra has only a face and two hands but no body. He is shown holding white lotuses in his two hands. He rides on a two or three wheeled chariot drawn by ten horses.

Maṇgala or Kuja has four hands, carrying the weapons mace and javelin in two, showing the Varada and Abhaya Mudrās with the other two. He rides on a ram.

Budha also has four hands, three of them wielding the weapons sword, shield and mace. The last hand shows the Varadamudrā. He rides on a lion or a chariot drawn by four horses.

Bṛhaspati, being the Guru, is shown holding a book and a rosary in his two hands. His chariot is golden and is driven by eight horses.

Śukra is also seated in a golden chariot drawn by eight horses or in a silver one drawn by ten horses. He has two hands holding a Nidhi (=treasure) and a book. Sometimes he is shown with four hands holding the staff, rosary and waterpot, the fourth exhibiting the Varadamudrā.

Śani rides in an iron chariot drawn by eight horses. He is more often shown as riding on a vulture. A buffalo also may be his mount. He holds the arrow, bow and javelin in three of his hands, the last hand being in the Varada Mudrā.

Rāhu is usually described as having only a face and Ketu is depicted like a serpent's tail. Iconographical works, however, describe them differently.

Rāhu may be shown riding a black lion or as seated on a Siṁhāsana (throne) or in a silver chariot drawn by eight horses. He may have two hands, the right hand carrying a woollen blanket and a book, the left hand being shown empty. If four hands are shown, they can carry sword, shield and lance, the fourth one being in Varada-mudrā.

Ketu has an ugly face and rides on a vulture. In his two arms he exhibits a mace and the Varadamudrā or Abhayamudrā.

All the Grahas have crowns and ear-rings. The eight grahas round the Sun always face him.

The planets are sometimes described as having connection with the incarnation of Lord Viṣṇu.

AṢṬADIKPĀLAKAS

They are the eight deities ruling over the eight quarters of the universe. Though frequently mentioned, they are rarely worshipped. They are mostly represented on the central panel of the ceiling in the Mahāmaṇḍapa (chief pavilion) of a temple.

Indra, Yama, Varuṇa and Kubera are the deities that rule over the east, south, west and north. The intermediate directions are ruled by Agni (south-east), Nirṛti (south-west), Vāyu (north-west) and Īśāna (north-east).

Indra, Yama, Varuṇa, Agni and Vāyu have already been dealt with in the fourth chapter on Vedic Gods.

Nirṛti is said to be the chief of the demons. He may be shown riding on a donkey, a lion or a man and surrounded by the demons and seven apsaras.

Kubera, the king of the Yakṣas (a kind of demigods) is famous as the lord of wealth. He is often depicted as riding on the shoulders of man or in a carriage drawn by men. Ram or elephant also can be his mount. Two Nidhis (personified treasures) are shown by his side.

Īśāna is an aspect of Śiva.

OTHER DEITIES

Among the subsidiary deities in Śiva temples, Kṣetrapāla occupies an important place. He is the chief guardian of the temple. His image is usually naked and aweinspring. He is worshipped first before commencing the regular service for the day. He seems to be an aspect of Bhairava.

Kṣetrapāla can also an independent deity with his own shrine, usually set up in the north-east corner of the town or the village. The shrine may face west or south, and rarely, east.

At the entrance of every temple are seen the Dvārapālakas ('guardian deities of the door'). They are invariably images in a standing posture. Their form and ornaments as also insignia vary according to the main deity whose temple they guard.

Practically every village has a goddess as its patron deity. Their number is legion. Almost all of them represent the terrible aspects of Pārvatī.

Sometimes diseases which bring havoc are deified. For instance, Śītalādevī is the goddess of smallpox. Or it can be the fear of the venomous reptiles that can create a deity like the Manasā (sister of Vāsuki, the serpent king), the goddess of snakes. Pangs of childbirth may have induced married women to hope for relief at the hands of Ṣaṣṭi, the deity that acts like a midwife and takes care of children!

10
FROM GODS TO GODHEAD

We have come a long way, passing through a veritable labyrinth, as it were, of the Hindu pantheon. The variety of the deities is as fascinating as it is bewildering. However, as long as we do not forget that the divine form we worship is an embodiment of the attributes that reveal the Supreme Principle in one way or the other, we are on safe ground. This knowledge should develop into an intense awareness of the Reality that is at the back of everything in the universe.

One more thing: This Reality, which is solidified consciousness as it were, can and does assume the forms of these various deities described here, in response to the wishes of the devotees who supplicate It. That innumerable mystics and seers have realized these forms is proof enough. Hence these deities are not just symbols but real.

Śiva is not just the god of destruction, dwelling on the Himālayas or the cremation ground. He is the embodiment of renunciation and destruction of all evil. He is the personification of contemplation and divine consciousness. He is 'the one Brahman, without a second, the All' (*Skandapurāṇa* 4.1.10.126).

Is Viṣṇu merely the lord of protection and preservation? He is the embodiment of the divine Principle that permeates the entire universe in which the world-play of creation, preservation and dissolution is enacted. He 'abideth in all.' He is 'all.' He assumes all forms (vide *Viṣṇupurāṇa* 1.12.71).

Similarly with the Mother Divine. Whether She is worshipped as the goddess of prosperity or propitiated out of fear for Her deadly dance of destruction, She is always the Power Supreme, the same as Brahman.

Again, Rāma is not just an ideal man but the personification of all virtues and the indweller of all beings. Kṛṣṇa is the highest ideal of divine love. His Viśvarūpa ('Universal Form') makes us exclaim, like Arjuna, 'Oh Lord! Thou art everything! Infinite in power and Infinite in prowess, Thou pervadest all' (*Bhagavad Gītā* 11.40).

But are we capable of perceiving this truth? As long as we are identified with our psycho-physical organism and feel its stifling limitations, we have to take the help of images and imagination. Is it not better to 'dream truer dreams,' as Swami Vivekananda puts it, than get stuck in morbid fancies of a mundane world? If images and imagination are adopted in the right spirit, they help us to evolve inwardly, leading us ultimately to the Infinite Spirit.

Notwithstanding all our logic and explanations, there still are academicians steeped in the Western traditions of comparative religion who discover fetishism or polytheism or henotheism or other 'isms' in our concept of gods and goddesses. These explanations or theories may hold good in the case of the Semitic religions but not with the religions of Āryan or Vedic origin. In Judaism the development was from the tribal gods called Molochs to the Supreme Molach. Each tribal god was identified with the tribe as its protector, as the embodiment of the tribal ego. In the internecine wars the victory of one tribe meant the breaking of the emblems or images of the god of that tribe and imposition of the god of the victorious tribe. Jehovah was the god that was finally victorious.

In Islam too we find the same trend. From the two hundred and odd gods in the Kaaba, Prophet Muhammad declared that Allah, one of them alone, was the only God and broke down the images of all the others. This act as also the well-known slogan of Islam, 'There is no God but Allah and Muhammad is His Prophet,' paved the way for the militarily victorious forces to break the objects of worship of the vanquished. Thus the journey from polytheism to monotheism lay through physical might rather than spiritual insight.

The development of the concept of God and gods among the Āryans was entirely on different lines. Even the anthropologists have agreed that the several gods of the Vedic pantheon were the presiding deities over forces of Nature. There was neither competition nor conflict among them, leading to displacement as among the Semitic gods. Gradually all these gods of natural forces were unified into one God the Supreme, who controls Nature and to whom Nature is a pointer. It is this that is signified by the well-known Vedic dictum, 'ekam sat viprāḥ bahudhā vadanti.'

So, there is in Hinduism no polytheism as understood by the Western thinkers. No doubt there is a tendency occasionally to exalt one god over all the others. This is due to Iṣṭaniṣṭhā or singular devotion to one's own Chosen Deity and hence, cannot be dubbed as 'henotheism' as Max Muller does.

The statement of Śrī Rāmakṛṣṇa that there are several ice-bergs in the boundless ocean clinches this issue very well. All the ice-bergs as also the ocean itself, are all WATER only! Once this Vedāntic background is grasped, the ideal of polytheism vanishes completely. The worship of Śiva, Śakti or Viṣṇu becomes the adoration the one Supreme Being who is Personal-Impersonal. The *Bhagavad Gītā* (4.11; 7.21) states the same truth in an unmistakable language.

This simile of the Supreme God or the Godhead as the infinite ocean can now be looked upon from a slightly different angle, useful to the Sādhakas or spiritual aspirants. The various gods can then be considered as Its waves. We, ordinary mortals that we are, with extraordinary attachment to our bodies and minds, are like bubbles. It is only when the bubble gets attached to the wave that it becomes conscious of its unity with the ocean. Upāsanā (worship and contemplation) of the various gods is thus the means by which we, the bubbles, become conscious of our divine heritage first, then, achieve the dissolution of our little selves in the Godhead, the universal Self. Since 'Knowledge is power,' a knowledge of these various gods of the Hindu faith will endow us with the power to know the Power behind them and BE FREE!

INDEX